he Name of Allah, Most Gracious, Most Merciful

Praise to Allah, Lord of the Universe.

May Peace and Prayers Be upon His

Final Prophet and Messenger.

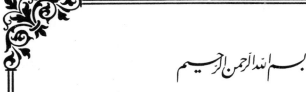

بِسْمِ اللهِ الرَّحْمَنِ الرَّحِيمِ

وَاعْتَصِمُوا بِحَبْلِ اللهِ جَمِيعًا وَلَا تَفَرَّقُوا وَاذْكُرُوا نِعْمَتَ اللهِ عَلَيْكُمْ إِذْ كُنتُمْ أَعْدَاءً فَأَلَّفَ بَيْنَ قُلُوبِكُمْ فَأَصْبَحْتُم بِنِعْمَتِهِ إِخْوَانًا وَكُنتُمْ عَلَىٰ شَفَا حُفْرَةٍ مِّنَ النَّارِ فَأَنقَذَكُم مِّنْهَا كَذَٰلِكَ يُبَيِّنُ اللهُ لَكُمْ ءَايَٰتِهِ لَعَلَّكُمْ تَهْتَدُونَ (آل عمران: ١٠٣)

And hold fast, all together, unto the bond with God, and do not draw apart from one another. And remember the blessings which God has bestowed upon you: how, when you were enemies, He brought your hearts together, so that through His blessing, you became brethren; and how, when you were on the brink of a fiery abyss, He saved you from it. In this way, God makes clear His messages unto you, that you find guidance.
(Qur'an 3: 103)

إِنَّ الَّذِينَ فَرَّقُوا دِينَهُمْ وَكَانُوا شِيَعًا لَّسْتَ مِنْهُمْ فِي شَيْءٍ إِنَّمَا أَمْرُهُمْ إِلَى اللهِ ثُمَّ يُنَبِّئُهُم بِمَا كَانُوا يَفْعَلُونَ (الأنعام: ١٥٩)

Verily, as for those who have broken the unity of their faith and have become sects—you have nothing to do with them. Their case rests with God and in time He will make them understand what they were doing.
(Qur'an 6: 159)

ISLAM AND ECONOMIC
DEVELOPMENT

ISLAMIZATION OF KNOWLEDGE — 14

Series Editor (in Pakistan): Zafar Ishaq Ansari

ISLAM
AND
ECONOMIC DEVELOPMENT

A Strategy for Development with Justice and Stability

M. UMER CHAPRA

**International Institute of Islamic Thought
and
Islamic Research Institute**

First published in Pakistan in 1993
by the International Institute of Islamic Thought, Islamabad
and Islamic Research Institute, Islamabad

c 1993   All rights reserved.
          International Institute of Islamic Thought,
          P.O. Box 1959,
          28, Main Double Road, F-10/2,
          Islamabad, Pakistan.
          Phone 92-51-851621   Fax: 92-51-280489

Cataloguing in Publication Data

Chapra, Muhammad Umer, 1933-
   Islam and Economic Development: A Strategy
   for Development with Justice and Stability/
   M. Umer Chapra
   (Islamization of Knowledge—14)

   Notes and References:pp. 133—154

ISBN 969-462-006-6

   1. Economic development — Religious aspects —
   Islam. 2. Economic development   338 .9 dc 20

Second Print in Malaysia
by;
PERCETAKAN ZAFAR SDN BHD
Kuala Lumpur
Tel: 03-6875725 Fax: 03-6875823

To my children
Maryam, Anas, Sumayyah and Ayman
and to all members
of the future generation
whose well-being
depends on the adoption of
the Islamic strategy
for development with justice and stability

Contents

PREFACE

Islamic Economics is now being taught in many universities around the Muslim world. Hence, the need has increased considerably for studies on different fields of economics to reflect the Islamic world-view. Since almost all Muslim countries fall within the category of developing countries, the need for a textbook on development economics has also been long felt. Although some textbooks have already become available on the subject, there is still need for a textbook that critically evaluates the neo-classical and socialist strategies for development to show why they cannot enable the Muslim countries to realise their own vision of development, and to help them formulate a strategy that is in harmony with the Islamic world-view and ideals. The present book, prepared on the suggestion of some friends, is an attempt to fulfil this need.

This book is the expanded version of a paper presented by me at a seminar on Islamic Economics held in Cairo in September 1988 under the auspices of the International Institute of Islamic Thought, Herndon, Va. (USA) and the al-Azhar University, Cairo (Egypt). The ideas expressed in this paper were derived from my book, *Islam and the Economic Challenge*, which was under preparation at that time, but which has now been published jointly by the Islamic Foundation, Leicester, U.K., and the International Institute of Islamic Thought. Consequently, the present work also reflects the ideas expressed in *Islam and the Economic Challenge* and draws freely on the materials contained in the chapters relevant to economic development. All this effort was directed to producing a book that would at once be of interest to all those who wish to understand the Islamic perspective on development and serve as a text-book for use by university students as well.

While all references have been given in the relevant notes, the references to the Qur'ān have been given within brackets immediately after the citation, the first number referring to the *sūrah* (chapter) and the second to the *āyah*(verse). The translation is my own; however, I have benefited from the translations of Abdullah Yusuf Ali, T.B. Irving, and Muhammad Asad.

I am particularly grateful to brother Dr. Zafar Ishaq Ansari for the encouragement he has provided in the preparation of this book and for the time he has spent in reading the manuscript and making a number of valuable suggestions for improvement. Hence, if the readers find this book clear and readable, a substantial part of the credit goes to him. I am also grateful to the Islamic Foundation and the International Institute of Islamic Thought for their permission to draw upon some chapters of my *Islam and the Economic Challenge*. I wish to take this opportunity to record my gratitude to Mr. Azmatullah Khan of the Islamic Foundation for his help in preparing the bibliography and to Mr. Mobin Ahmad for the secretarial assistance he has so efficiently provided.

M. Umer Chapra

Riyadh
9 Rajab 1412
13 January 1992

FOREWORD

One of the dominant features of the present century is the almost intermittent rivalry and competition between capitalism and communism. Each of the two doctrines did its best to make its vision of socio-economic life prevail in, let alone establish its hegemony over, the whole world. Thanks to the prominence of these twin ideologies over a vast stretch of time, most human beings entertained for long the belief that they had no other option but to choose one of the two.

This was natural since no other politico-economic systems were effectively in operation in the world; nor were the votaries of any other doctrine engaged in propagating their doctrine to all mankind.

The first half of the present century saw a great majority of Muslims languishing under foreign tutelage. The few Muslim countries that were politically independent were steeped in backwardness as were the Muslim countries under foreign control. As a consequence, the Muslims were in no position to play an effective role on the stage of history. In such a circumstance it was not surprising that the Muslims should also feel attracted to the ideologies which had been accepted by the majority of mankind. Nor was it surprising that many Muslims should also be inclined to believe, like the rest of mankind, that their choice was confined to the dominant systems of the time.

Such a trend of thought, however, was not quite in tune with the genius of the Muslim *ummah* which had been taught that Islam's validity was not time-bound. Hence, even in the most depressing decades of the present century, we find powerful Muslim voices affirming Islam's self-sufficiency, its all-pervading character, its timeless relevance, and its innate soundness. Although such voices rose from all parts of the world, perhaps the most powerful voice was the one from the South Asian Subcontinent, the voice of Muhammad Iqbal (d. 1938).

For quite a while the Muslim statements which challenged the hegemony of the dominant secular ideologies might have had a ring of oddness. To claim that Islam was intrinsically superior to the contemporary systems and that Islam alone could provide the panacea for the sufferings of all mankind might have appeared little more than empty, idealistic bombast. But gradually an increasing number of people — both Muslims and others — awoke to the fact that the systems currently in vogue were, to say the least, not an unmixed blessing. In fact by the Second World War it became evident that the dominant materialist spirit and orientation of the contemporary civilization had brought untold misery to mankind. The rank brutality of the modern man, his conspicuous indifference to the sufferings of others, his potential to wreak destruction on a mass scale, his excessive immersion in the pursuit of pleasure, his growing indifference to the higher urges of human nature, and his loss of direction and purpose were too evident to be perceived by all, even by men of very ordinary intellect. Hence many of those who had believed in man's inexorable progress were disillusioned. In this changed context, the Islamic claims began to make greater sense.

As the prospect of the political liberation of Muslim lands seemed to hover over the horizon, Islam's self-sufficiency began to be asserted by Muslim leaders, thinkers, ideologues and litterateurs with increasing fervour and vehemence. Around the middle of the century when political liberation became a reality for some Muslim countries, and a clear prospect for the rest, this trend assumed even greater importance and urgency.

One of the fields in which Islamic self-affirmation has been most conspicuous is that of economic doctrine and practice; in other words, the Muslims have become eager and insistent on building an economy consistent with Islamic values and norms.

This should not have come as a surprise to anyone for there was a great deal in both capitalism and communism which had anathematized the Muslims. The Muslims did not feel comfortable with the crass individualism which manifested itself in the cut-throat competition characterizing the capitalist system. Nor were the Muslims impressed by the smug complacence of the exponents of capitalism who argued that an unbridled pursuit of self-interest would necessarily lead — thanks to the operation of some "invisible hand" — to the well-being of all. Muslim religious conscience felt particularly ill at ease with interest, the backbone of the capitalist economy. The Muslims could not appreciate that interest, which the Qur'ān had categorically denounced, could be a blessing for man's economic life. At the same time, the Muslims also felt abhorred by the communist doctrine which envisaged total abolition of private property. They shared, on the whole, the Western liberal distrust of the communist scheme of things. They were no less critical than the Western liberals of its potential for excessive regimentation, its propensity to smother individual freedom and initiative, its being discordant with human nature, and, at least in the long run, its being an unworkable proposition from the economic point of view.

Even in the forties, therefore, the espousal of an Islamic economic system was not uncommon in the writings of Muslim scholars. Subsequently, in the post-independence period the desire for the establishment of an Islamic system of life, which would naturally also embrace the economic sector of life, became stronger. The desire for building economic institutions in accordance with Islamic principles, (such as interest-free financial institutions, the governmental collection of *zakāh*, etc.), gradually led to the emergence of an intellectual movement. As a consequence, the questions pertaining to economic matters began to be increasingly discussed at an academic level from an Islamic perspective. During the last few decades a growing number of Muslim economists, mostly trained in the Western intellectual tradition, have emphasized the need for a distinctly Islamic approach to economic questions. This has generated the concern for developing a new approach to economics, and in the case of quite a few, the concern for developing a new academic discipline generally called Islamic Economics Dr. Chapra is in the vanguard of this movement and is among the few scholars who have richly contributed to this academic effort.

Even in the early part of his life Dr. Chapra had faced the question which the Muslims have faced throughout the present century, but especially in the post-independence period: should they look up to the capitalist "West" or to the communist "East" for inspiration and guidance in their effort to build the institutions of their newly-established, independent states? Or should they mainly depend, instead, on their own intellectual resources?

In his student days, Dr. Chapra had made an effort to study the teachings of Islam pertaining to economic life. Not long after his return to Pakistan from USA in 1961, Dr. Chapra joined the Central Institute of Islamic Research and spent two years systematically exploring the ideas and principles enshrined in the Islamic tradition which, in his view, could serve as the intellectual premises of a healthy economic system. This effort, which was further refined and matured by subsequent study and reflection, led to his first book, *The Economic System of Islam — a Discussion of its Goals and Nature* (London, 1970).

In 1964 Dr. Chapra proceded to U.S.A. After teaching Economics in American universities for a few years, Dr. Chapra joined the Saudi Arabian Monetary Fund as its Economic Adviser. His long association with this organization gave Dr. Chapra a first-hand acquaintance with the complex operational aspects of money and finance in the present times. However, even though he has been concerned, by way of professional duty, with matters relating to monetary policy, Dr. Chapra always remained a scholar. He never ceased to study and reflect over the characteristics of a monetary system, in fact, of an economic system as such that might be at once truly Islamic and contemporaneously viable. Dr. Chapra was convinced that a just monetary system could be established only on the economic principles of Islam. The doctrines which had come to dominate the world scene — capitalism, socialism, communism and the doctrine of welfare state — were all too flawed to guide man in his effort to establish an economic system that would combine economic progress with justice and equity and ensure higher standards of living go hand in hand with high standards of morality. This was the focus of Dr. Chapra's thought-provoking book, *Towards a Just Monetary System* (Leicester, 1985).

This major work was followed after a few years by another, and perhaps an even more stimulating, more mature, and more thoroughgoing work, *Islam and the Economic Challenge* (Leicester, 1992). These works, in addition to the several research papers relating to Islamic economy, have made Dr. Chapra one of the most profound representatives of the school of thought generally called "Islamic Economics". Those who have read Dr. Chapra's writings have found him both profound and provocative, and certainly felicitous and engaging.

This writer, whose friendship with Dr. Chapra goes back to the fifties, has had the pleasure of keeping track of his academic work. Throughout the last twenty five years his writings have displayed a high standard of scholarship combined with courage of conviction. When Dr. Chapra's first book and his early papers on the Islamic economic system were published, socialism was very much in fashion. Dr. Chapra's writings, however, envisaged an Islamic economic system which rests on intellectual premises significantly at variance with those of both capitalism and socialism. During this period — the middle seventies — the present writer has had occasion to hear harsh critical comments about Dr. Chapra's ideas which bordered on disparagement: "Dr. Chapra's Islamic economic system is nothing but capitalism, duly sanctified by recourse to Islamic trappings". Such comments notwithstanding, Dr. Chapra firmly stood his ground.

Now in the 1990s, we live in a world with a different climate of opinion. The idol of socialism, which once had hosts of fanatic devotees all around the world, has been shattered to pieces and has apparently been consigned to the dust-bin of history. (For this author's somewhat different view, see his 'Foreword' to Tahir Amin, *Nationalism and Internationalism in Three Traditions: Liberalism, Marxism and Islam*, Islamabad, 1991, p. xi). As a consequence, in recent years capitalism has gained close to universal respectability. It is being played up as the zenith of man's striving for good life; as the very "end of history". It is significant that in this changed climate of opinion, we find Dr. Chapra once again swimming against the current. Perhaps to the surprise of many, Dr. Chapra's recent writings present a sustained argument to establish that capitalism, even in its present, reformed shape, is riddled with too many basic flaws to be capable of providing the foundations of a just socio-economic order.

Coming to the present book, Dr. Chapra has taken up a question of vital importance for all human beings, but specially for the present-day Muslims. The question relates to the current models of economic development evolved in the West. Are these essentially good models, models that will indeed lead mankind to happiness and justice? Or, can a better model, inspired by the teachings of Islam, be offered to mankind as a workable alternative?

It is evident that this is one of the burning questions of the day for the Muslims who are naturally desirous of overcoming their present under-development. Perhaps it is no exaggeration to say that Dr. Chapra's book is the first serious and significant effort to develop the intellectual blueprints of an alternate, Islamic model of economic development. Dr. Chapra is far too humble, and far too mature to believe that he has said the last word on the subject. However, perhaps few readers will dispute that in this book he does indeed provide ample food for thought and that he marks a significant milestone in developing the contours of an Islamic development strategy.

As the work goes to the press, the debt we owe at least to those who have significantly contributed to the preparation and publication of this work needs to be acknowledged. My colleague, Mr. Muhammad Naeem, Assistant Editor of *Islamic Studies*, did an excellent job of technical editing. His meticulousness is matched only by a sharply perceptible eye for even the most trivial flaw. Mr. Tahir Farkhan Ahmad very ably and painstakingly composed this book, enduring with remarkable patience both the present writer's and Mr. Naeem's desire to produce, as far as humanly possible, a flawless work. Mr. Zafar Ali, the Manager of the Islamic Research Institute Press, extended his ungrudging cooperation to ensure an elegant production. Mr. Imtiaz Zafar, a lecturer in the Da'wah Academy, International Islamic University, Islamabad kindly prepared the index. All of these deserve our sincere thanks. Last, but not the least, is the gratitude we owe the learned author. Dr. Chapra has done a singular favour by making this fine book available for publication to one of his long-time friends, a favour for which he cannot be thanked enough. May Allah bless him.

Islamabad
July, 1993

ZAFAR ISHAQ ANSARI

INTRODUCTION

All Muslim countries fall within the category of developing countries even though some of them are relatively rich while others are extremely poor. Most of these countries, particularly the poorer ones, like other developing countries, are also beset with a number of extremely difficult problems. One of these problems is their macroeconomic imbalance reflected in high rates of unemployment and inflation, excessive balance of payments deficits, continued exchange rate depreciation and heavy debt burden. The other problem is the extreme inequality of income and wealth among the different classes of each country, as well as between different Muslim countries. Consequently, while even the basic needs of a considerable portion of the population remain unsatisfied, the rich and the upper middle classes live in great affluence. This tends to corrode the fabric of social solidarity and serves as one of the prime causes of socio-political instability.

Given this scenario, what is indispensable for the Muslim countries is not just a reasonably high rate of growth in aggregate output. They also need to substantially reduce their macroeconomic imbalances and socio-economic inequalities. Without this reduction in imbalances and inequalities, even the continued growth of output and the socio-political health and stability of these countries will, in the ultimate, be seriously jeopardised. The Muslim countries like all other developing countries are, therefore, looking for a development strategy that would help them accelerate growth with justice and reduced instability.

Since Islamic resurgence is gaining momentum in almost all Muslim countries, five basic questions arise in the mind. The first question is about the kind of development that Islam envisages. The second and the third questions are whether this kind of development can be realised with the secular approach of those who believe either in the market system or socialism or with strategies formulated by development economists within the framework of these two systems. If not, then the fourth question is about the strategy that the *Shari'ah* (Islamic teachings) can help the Muslim countries formulate in order to actualise development of the kind that Islam envisages with substantially reduced macroeconomic imbalances. If a successful strategy can be formulated within the framework of the *Shari'ah*, then the fifth question is as to why the Muslim countries have so far failed to formulate and implement such a strategy. Each of these five questions has been discussed in a separate chapter in this book. The concluding chapter wraps up the entire discussion so as to enable the reader to get a gist of the whole analysis.

ONE

THE KIND OF DEVELOPMENT

STABILITY AND SOCIO-ECONOMIC GOALS

If economic resources at the disposal of human beings were unlimited, everybody would be able to get whatever he or she desired and there would be no discussion of either their growth or their allocation and distribution. Resources are, however, limited. This scarcity, on the one hand, necessitates the expansion and development of economic resources and, on the other hand, imposes two constraints on their use. The first of these is that relative stability must be maintained through the attainment of an equilibrium between the supply of resources and the claims on them so as to avoid prolonged macro-economic imbalances and the problems associated with such imbalances. However, every society also professes certain socio-economic goals. Therefore, the second constraint is that stability must be attained in such a manner that the goals of the society concerned are also optimally realised. It is generally agreed that stability and goal-realisation are both necessary for the continued health and development of an economy.

The simultaneous realisation of stability as well as the socio-economic goals of the society require a strategy and there may be a number of strategies that could be considered for this purpose. All the available strategies may not, however, be successful. This brings into focus the choice of an effective strategy. Since it is an economic system which concerns itself with the development of a proper strategy, it is not possible to avoid a discussion of the choice of an appropriate economic system in any discussion of economic development.

GOALS, STRATEGY, AND WORLD-VIEW

The goals of an economic system are essentially determined by its world-view, which discusses questions about how the universe came into existence, the meaning and purpose of human life, the ultimate ownership and objective of the limited resources at the disposal of human beings, and the relationship of human beings to each other (involving their rights and responsibilities) and to their environment. For example, if the universe has come into existence by itself, then human beings are not accountable to anyone and are free to live as they please. Their purpose in life would then be to seek maximum pleasure, irrespective of how this is realised and how it affects others or their environment. The serving of self-interest and the survival of the fittest would then seem to be the most logical norms of behaviour. If it is believed that human beings are merely pawns on the chessboard of history and their life is determined by external forces over which they have no control, they are, then, not responsible for what goes on around them and need have no qualms about the prevailing inequities.

However, if human beings and what they possess have been created by the Supreme Being and they are accountable to Him, then they may not consider themselves either absolutely free to behave as they please or helpless pawns on the chessboard of history, unconcerned about the direction in which history is moving. Rather they have a mission to perform and must use the limited resources and treat each other and their environment in a way that would help fulfil their mission.

The strategy to realise these goals would also then be determined by the world-view. For example, if the survival of the fittest is an acceptable norm of behaviour and if the economic system is merely concerned with the function of bringing about economic stability in a smooth manner, then the strategy would not be the same as that of a system which has to realise certain goals along with stability. If both the goals and stability are to be realised without unduly sacrificing the freedom of the individual, then the strategy would be different from that of a system which does not place a high value on individual freedom.

Both the goals and the strategy of an economic system are, therefore, the logical outcome of its world-view. It may, of course, be possible for an economic system to derive its goals from one world-view and its strategy from another. For example, the goals may be derived from a religious world-view that considers all human beings members of a single brotherhood and holds them responsible for the plight of others, but the strategy may be derived from world-views that stand for survival of the fittest and class conflict — world-views that implicitly negate the brotherhood and well-being of the humanity collectively. In this case, there will be a conflict between the goals and the strategy. This conflict will not only make it difficult for the system to realise its goals but will give rise to a number of other difficult and insoluble socio-economic problems.

Therefore, in any discussion of economic development in Muslim countries, it is imperative to look at the Islamic world-view and the goals that conform to such a world-view and the kind of development that this implies. This will help us examine, in chapters 2 and 3, whether the strategies of the market system, or of socialism and development economics which being based on a secular world-view, are in sharp conflict with that of Islam, can help Muslim countries develop a strategy that would enable them to realise development of the kind consistent with the Islamic world-view. This is followed, in chapter 4, by a discussion of the strategy that the Muslim world needs for this purpose.

ISLAMIC WORLD-VIEW

The Islamic world-view is based on three fundamental concepts. These are: *tawḥīd* (Oneness and Unity of God), *khilāfah* (vicegerency of human beings), and *'adālah* (justice). *Tawḥīd* is the most important of these concepts because the other two are its logical derivatives. *Tawḥīd* implies that the universe has been consciously designed and created by the Supreme Being, Who is One and Unique, and that it did not come into existence by chance or accident (Qur'ān, 3:191, 38:27, and 23:15). Everything created by Him has a purpose. It is this purpose which gives meaning and significance to the existence of the universe, of which human beings are a part. This being the case, human beings by virtue of the fact that they have been endowed with freewill, rationality, and moral consciousness combined with an inherent God-consciousness, are required to live in exclusive worship and obedience to the Supreme Being. Thus *tawḥīd* is not merely recognition of reality, but an active response to it.

The human being is the Supreme Being's *khalīfah* or vicegerent on earth (Qur'ān, 2:30, 6:165, 35:39, 38:28, and 57:7), and the resources at his disposal are a trust (Qur'ān, 57:7). Since God has created the human beings, He alone possesses the perfect knowledge of their nature and their strengths and weaknesses, and He alone is capable of providing them with guidance that would be in harmony with their nature and needs. In His infinite mercy, God has provided this guidance — consisting of beliefs, values, and laws of behaviour — through a chain of Messengers, including Abraham, Moses, Jesus and Muḥmmad, may the peace and blessings of God be on them all. Although human beings are free to accept or reject this guidance, they can attain true well-being (*falāḥ*) only by implementing it in their own lives as well as in their societies. As His vicegerents, human beings are accountable to Him and will be rewarded or punished in the Hereafter in accordance with whether they do or do not live in this world in conformity with the guidance provided by Him.

Since everyone, rather than any single privileged person or members of a particular race or group or country, is a *khalīfah*, *khilāfah* essentially stands for the fundamental unity and brotherhood of mankind. This brotherhood would remain a hollow concept devoid of all substance if it is not accompanied by *'adālah* (justice). Establishment of justice has, therefore, been declared by the Qur'ān to be one of the primary objectives which God's Messengers seek to achieve (Qur'ān, 57:25). In fact, the Qur'ān places justice "nearest to piety" (5:8) in terms of its importance in the Islamic faith. Piety, or moral development, implies closeness to God attained through the faithful implementation of all values and establishment of all institutions prescribed by Him through the Qur'ān and the *Sunnah* (the Prophet's sayings and actions), and is thus extemely important because it serves as a springboard for all rightful actions, including the establishment of justice.

GOALS OF ISLAM (*MAQĀSID AL-SHARĪ'AH*)

This intense commitment of Islam to brotherhood and justice makes the well-being (*falāḥ*) of all human beings the principal goal of Islam.[1] This well-being includes physical satisfaction because mental peace and happiness can be achieved only by means of a balanced realisation of both the material and spiritual needs of the human personality. Therefore, mere maximisation of total output cannot be the goal of a Muslim society. Maximisation of output must be accompanied by ensuring efforts directed to spiritual health at the inner core of human consciousness, and justice and fair play at all levels of human interaction. Only development of this kind would be in conformity with the *maqāsid al-Sharī'ah* or goals of the *Sharī'ah* (referred to hereafter as the *maqāsid* or the goals).

While satisfaction of the spiritual needs requires moral development, satisfaction of the material needs requires the development of all human and material resources in such a just manner that the needs of all human beings are adequately fulfilled and there is an equitable distribution of income and wealth. However, since Islam proscribes begging as it is inconsistent with the inherent dignity of man as the *khalīfah* of God, it is the personal obligation of every person who is physically and mentally fit, to support himself and his family. This may not be possible unless facilities are provided for training him to become more productive through the development of his abilities and, also, unless there exist opportunities for self-employment and for working on wages.

It is, therefore, the collective obligation of the Muslim society to ensure proper training and optimal employment. Moreover, since one of the principal teachings of the *Sharī'ah* is not to harm others nor to reciprocate the harm done by others,[2] the prevention of excessive depletion of non-renewable natural resources and pollution of the environment, which harm both the present and the future generations, are also an individual as well as a collective obligation of all Muslims. Hence, 'development with justice' could be considered to have been realised if the dictates of *khilāfah* and *'adālah* are satisfied through the need-fulfilment of all, equitable distribution of income and wealth, full employment, and environmental protection.

BASIC THESIS

While secular societies continue to belittle the need for moral development, all of them now profess commitment to development with justice. It is the basic thesis of this book that even material development with justice is not possible without moral development. The rationale for this contention is that development with justice requires an 'efficient' and equitable use of all resources and both 'efficiency' and 'equity' can neither be defined nor actualised without the injection of a moral dimension into economic pursuits.

EFFICIENCY AND EQUITY

Efficiency and equity have been defined in a number of ways. From the perspective of the *Sharī'ah*, the most appropriate definitions would seem to be those that would help realise the Islamic vision of development. Hence, optimum efficiency may be said to have been achieved in the allocation of resources if the maximum feasible quantity of need-satisfying goods and services is produced with a reasonable degree of economic stability and a sustainable rate of growth.

The test of such efficiency lies in the ability to attain a socially more acceptable result without creating prolonged macroeconomic imbalances and without unduly depleting non-renewable resources or damaging the environment. Optimum equity may be said to have been attained in the distribution of resources if the needs of all individuals are adequately satisfied and there is an equitable distribution of income and wealth without adversely affecting the motivation for work, saving, investment, and enterprise.

The definitions for efficiency and equity given above, however, cannot exist in a moral vacuum.[3] This is because the most important principle of physical science is that matter can neither be created nor destroyed. Total output will thus always be equal to total input in physical terms. The correct definition of efficiency would hence be, as Frank Knight has rightly argued, the ratio between useful output and total output or input, and not between total output and total input.[4] This means that a measure of 'usefulness' is needed to measure efficiency.

If profit-maximisation is considered to be a measure of usefulness, then all equity-related goals must be treated as residuals and cannot be a part of the economic model. If, however, need-fulfilment is considered to be a measure of usefulness, then the satisfaction of all wants according to individual preferences cannot be a goal of the economic system. Wants must, therefore, be classified according to their ability to satisfy needs.

This requires a socially-agreed filter and a strong motivation on the part of individuals to abide by the verdict of this filter. Similarly, it is not possible to talk meaningfully about an equitable distribution of income without looking at the needs of all individuals and families and determining the kind of income distribution and socio-economic organisation that would lead to the fulfilment of these needs. Any socio-economic organisation that does not lead to an income distribution that satisfies the basic needs of all has to be regarded as necessarily inequitable.

ELEMENTS OF A SUCCESSFUL STRATEGY

This indicates that if a strategy is to be successful in realising optimum efficiency and equity in the use of scarce resources, it must consist of three important elements: (a) a filter mechanism to enable individuals to choose between the unlimited use of resources in such a way that the aggregate claims do not exceed the supply, and the socio-economic goals of the system are also realised; (b) a motivating mechanism, to induce individuals to put in their best in conformity with the dictates of such a filter mechanism, irrespective of whether this serves their own interest or the interest of the society; and (c) socio-economic restructuring to help transfer scarce resources from one use to another until optimum efficiency and equity are realised.

The proposed strategy cannot be equipped with these three indispensable elements without injecting a moral dimension into the economic system. Any economic system which has secular answers to the metaphysical questions, raised earlier, about the meaning and purpose of life, the ultimate ownership and objective of the limited resources, and the rights and obligations of all individuals in society, can provide neither a proper filter mechanism nor an effective motivating system and socio-economic restructuring. This will become clear in the next chapter.

NEED FOR A NEW STRATEGY

Muslim countries have, nevertheless, tried to pursue so far the development strategies provided by Western development economics. Development economics, however, does not have a separate identity of its own. It has been conceived within the secular and this-worldly perspective of both the market system and socialism. Their problems have, however, been aggravated and when Muslims tried to implement Western development strategies, they moved farther and farther away from the realisation of the *maqāṣid*.

It is, therefore, important to see why the pursuit of development with strategies based on a secular and this-worldly world-view was bound either to frustrate their efforts to realise development with justice or to lead to an accentuation of their macroeconomic imbalances. The following chapter, therefore, looks at the world-view and strategy of both the market system and socialism and discusses the adverse effects of these on justice. This will prepare the ground for a discussion of the strategies proposed by development economics and Islam in the two chapters that follow.

★★★

Two

CAN SECULARISM FOSTER JUST DEVELOPMENT?

Secularism is the dominant world-view in the Western world and, as a result of the Western political, intellectual and economic domination over other countries, it has also become the prevalent world-view in the Third World. It is a by-product of the Enlightenment movement, which tried to undermine the hold of religion as a collective force in society and placed great confidence in the ability of reason to discover ultimate metaphysical truths as well as prescribe values for ordering human life. While it does not necessarily deny the existence of a Supreme Being, it assumes that His existence does not carry any significance for human life. The business of life is conducted on the assumption that there is no life after death and that there is no accountability before the Supreme Being. Unlike religion, the dominant world-view concerns itself with only the material aspects of life, and its essential principle is that human well-being can be brought about only by material means.

The deep-seated dislike for, or indifference to, religion in the modern West made it averse to value judgements based on moral considerations. Human actions were to be judged, instead, in the light of a stark utilitarianism according to which 'right' and 'wrong', 'good' and 'evil' were to be determined by the sensations of 'pleasure' and 'pain'. Whatever gave pleasure was good and whatever caused pain was evil. A logical basis was thus provided, at least psychologically, for the single-minded pursuit of wealth and sensual pleasures.

This gave rise to the concept of 'economic man', which has served as the kingpin of modern economics. Self-interest was the only well-spring of his action. Consumption was the highest purpose of his life, the supreme source of happiness, and the ultimate justification for all his effort. Maximising earnings and want satisfaction became supreme virtues. Everything done by the individual towards this end was justified. He should, therefore, be left free to serve his self-interest. Any talk of the 'rights of man' was plain nonsense.[1] Economic life was conceived as an arena of competition regulated by a free market system which would ensure the survival of the fittest. Social Darwinism, thus, crept into economics.

INEQUITY OF THE MARKET STRATEGY

It is this secularist world-view that has served as the fountainhead of capitalism which, in its classical *laissez-faire* sense, does not exist anywhere. It has been modified over the centuries and is now generally referred to by the less opprobrious term of the market system, which refers to reformed capitalism and embodies the principles of both *laissez-faire* capitalism and the welfare state. Its world-view is, nevertheless, as secular as that of *laissez-faire* capitalism. Its goals are, however, more humanitarian. To realise these goals it has advocated greater government intervention in the market to correct some of the shortcomings of the *laissez-faire* model, and to offset, at least partly, some of its inequities.

Nevertheless, the charismatic appeal of the original model has continued. This appeal has gained further strength from the failure of socialism, the disenchantment with a large government role in the economy, and the backlash against the welfare state. Calls have been intensified in recent years from both intellectual and political platforms for liberalism, or a return, as nearly as possible, to the classical model with 'minimum' government intervention. This call, at present, tends to dominate the thinking and economic policies of not only the Western industrial countries, but also of a substantial part of the Third World and the now-liberalising Communist countries. It is hence desirable to understand the rationale of the system and to see whether it is logically possible for this system to realise efficiency, which is taken for granted as its hallmark, and equity which, as many economists have always acknowledged, it cannot realise.

Within the perspective of the prevailing *zeitgeist*, which recognises a certain allocative and distributive role for the government to realise socially-desired goals, the market system may be distinguished by its emphasis on:

(i)   unhindered individual freedom to pursue pecuniary self-interest and to own and manage private property;

(ii)   accelerated wealth expansion and maximum production and want-satisfaction in accordance with individual preferences; and

(iii)   primary role for market forces in the allocation and distribution of resources, and 'minimum' role for government intervention or collective value judgements.

THE RATIONALE

The pursuit of unlimited self-interest, which the market system stands for, had a religious stigma attached to it. Unless this was removed, it would not have received the social blessings it needed in a Christian society, which was committed to the safeguard of social interest and the realisation of its humanitarian goals. This was done by Adam Smith. He argued that the serving of self-interest by everyone would ultimately serve the social interest.

The rationale behind this assertion of Adam Smith was that the desire to serve self-interest will induce the individual to be most efficient. Competition will, however, serve as a constraint on his greed and prevent him from exceeding the limits of social interest. Consumers will try to buy at the lowest price whatever is in accordance with their preferences. These preferences will become known to the producers by the votes they cast in the market place through their willingness to pay the market price determined by the interaction of supply and demand. Producers will try to produce at the lowest cost whatever the consumers prefer, so as to maximise their profits. This behaviour of both consumers and producers will ensure efficiency as well as equity. Therefore, individuals should be given maximum freedom to serve their self-interest through the maximisation of their income, consumption and wealth. The government should intervene only to the extent to which it was necessary to ensure competition and orderly markets and to offset market failure in attaining the desired outcomes in resources use.

Within the perspective of the above rationale, the terms efficiency and equity do not have a direct relationship with the egalitarian objectives of removing poverty, fulfilling needs, attaining full employment, and reducing inequalities of income and wealth. It was assumed that these objectives will also be realised as a 'necessary' concomitant of efficiency and equity brought about by the competitive equilibrium. Any outside intervention to change the status quo would necessarily lead to results which are less efficient and less equitable. The only acceptable way to change the status quo was within the value-neutral framework of Pareto optimality — to make some people 'better off' without making anyone 'worse off'.

Thus, the filter mechanism in the market system consists of market-determined prices. These, it is argued, serve as signals to both consumers and producers and trigger the transfer of resources from one use to another until the supply has become equal to the demand. Since only those who consider the goods or service 'necessary' will be willing to pay the market-determined price, market forces will automatically determine the 'necessary' from the 'unnecessary' and the 'equitable' from the 'inequitable' use of resources without resort to collective value judgements or government intervention.

The primary motivating force in this entire process is self-interest. The serving of self-interest by everyone in a free and competitive market environment serves the social interest by leading to a most 'efficient' and 'equitable' distribution.[2] Trying to do this in any other way would require value judgement which is an anathema within the framework of the secularist Enlightenment philosophy. The market system thus sidesteps the crucial issues of ethics and socio-economic justice by asserting that market forces are sufficient to keep self-interest within the bounds of social well-being.

UNREALISTIC ASSUMPTIONS

A number of assumptions are implicitly made in the above reasoning. These are, however, normally not spelled out clearly in the economic writings. Some of these assumptions are:

Harmony between Individual and Social Interest

Firstly, it is assumed that everything that is in the interest of the individual is also in the interest of the society and there is no possibility of conflict between the two. This is a false assumption. The two interests need not always be in harmony, particularly when there is nothing in a secular environment to motivate the utility-maximising consumer and the profit-maximising producer to serve the social interest when this is in conflict with his personal interest. For example, a substantial reduction in luxury consumption of the rich is in the interest of increased savings and investment and of bringing about general need-fulfilment and full employment, but may not necessarily be in the immediate interest of the rich. Similarly, avoiding the pollution of a country's rivers is in the interest of the society, but it might not necessarily satisfy the immediate, this-worldly self-interest of producers because it raises costs and reduces profits; market forces would tend to benefit those who avoid such costs. Market solutions to these problems may not always be feasible or successful because, while the rise in cost brought about by market solutions may not impose a significant constraint on the rich, it may considerably hurt the poor.

Individual Preferences Reflect Social Priorities

Secondly, it is assumed that even in a secular system based on utilitarian values, the self-interested sovereign consumer would confine his claims on resources only to need-satisfaction. This assumption has also proved to be false. Without the restraint that commitment to moral values promotes in the use of resources, the votes cast in the market place may not reflect social priorities. Why would the rich abstain from diverting scarce resources from the need-fulfilment of others to the satisfaction of their preference for prestige symbols, particularly when the consumer culture has created an atmosphere of competition for their acquisition? If the pace-setters in the society have them, others also consider them indispensable even if they cannot afford them and have to resort to unscrupulous means to acquire them.

Equal Distribution

Thirdly, it is assumed that there is an equal distribution of income and wealth because only an equal distribution would give everyone an equal weight in influencing the decision-making process of the market in a secular environment where moral values do not serve as a constraint on resource use. However, since there are substantial inequalities of income and wealth, and since the rich are also able to have a far greater access to credit, they are able to buy whatever they wish at the prevailing prices, and to tilt the allocation of resources in their favour. Accordingly, as Samuelson has rightly indicated, market forces will only lead to "starving couples; to malnourished children who grow up to produce malnourished children; to perpetuation of Lorenz curves of great inequality of income and wealth for generations or forever."[3]

Prices Reflect Urgency of Wants

Fourthly, it is assumed that the willingness of consumers to pay the market price reflects the urgency of wants. This is also false because even though the urgency for milk is the same for all children, irrespective of whether they are rich or poor, the amount of dollar votes that a poor family is able to cast for milk is not the same as those that a rich family is able to cast for status symbols. Hence Arthur Okun has rightly observed that markets "award prizes that allow the big winners to feed their pets better than the losers can feed their children."[4]

Market Imperfections

Fifthly, it is also assumed that there is perfect competition with many buyers, many sellers, no barriers to entry and perfect knowledge. Perfect competition has, however, remained an unrealised dream and is likely to remain so, particularly because of the tendency under capitalism towards the promotion of big business and concentration of wealth and power.

The innumerable imperfections that exist in the market thwart the efficient operation of market forces and produce deviations from the ideally competitive marginal cost pricing, thus leading to prices that do not reflect real costs or benefits. Hence, while prices are not, by themselves, capable of bringing about a socially-desired allocation and distribution of resources, they would tend to be more so if they do not even reflect real costs and benefits.

SOCIAL DARWINISM

The price system thus leads to social Darwinism in resource allocation and distribution. The rich are able, by the sheer weight of their purchasing power, to get scarce national resources diverted to the production or import of luxuries and false symbols of prestige which do not fall within the category of needs. The situation is worsened by value-free advertising, which promotes the sale of status symbols, and the relatively easy access of the rich to the enormous financial resources of the banking system through credit. The result is that in the market economies, as rightly indicated by Tawney, a "part of the goods which are annually produced, and which are called wealth is, strictly speaking, waste because it consists of articles which though reckoned as part of the income of the nation, either should not have been produced until other articles had been produced in sufficient abundance or should not have been produced at all."[5]

CRISIS OF THE WELFARE STATE

The inequities generated by *laissez-faire* capitalism gave rise to the welfare state, which provided a ray of hope on the capitalist horizon. The welfare state was not, however, based on a world-view different from that of capitalism. All it did was to combine the price mechanism with a greater role of the state in the economy to ensure higher economic growth and greater stability and equity. The unprecedented growth during the two decades of the fifties and the sixties and the continually rising welfare spending by the governments have, however, failed to remove poverty, fulfil needs and reduce inequalities even in the world's richest countries. In fact, as Adelman and Morris have convincingly shown on the basis of a cross-section of data, "development is accompanied by an absolute as well as a relative decline in the average income of the poor."[6]

But growth has now faltered and unemployment has become a chronic, long-run problem. Economic instability has also heightened and is increasingly reflected in the commodity, stock, and foreign exchange markets. There seems to be no hope of faster growth and full employment in the near future without rekindling inflation and aggravating macroeconomic imbalances and economic instability. Moreover, public sector spending to provide welfare services to the rich and the poor alike — the only feasible option within the framework of value-neutrality — has in fact helped the rich more than the poor because of their larger purchases and their easier access to facilities.[7] Inequalities of income and wealth have also risen in spite of progressive taxation and welfare state services. This indicates that the strategy of adding just a greater government role to *laissez-faire* capitalism to realise its goals has proved to be ineffective.

The welfare state is now facing a crisis. While its goals have remained unrealised, it is under pressure to roll back its frontiers as a result of the huge budgetary deficits that the welfare states are now facing. The primary reason for these deficits is that the imperative of operating within the framework of Pareto optimality deprived the welfare state of socially-agreed moral criteria for evaluating the various claims on its resources. It was thus unable to offset the increased public sector spending for both growth and welfare by a reduction in other claims on resources. This led to an avalanche of claims. The satisfaction of these claims by means of deficit financing, excessive credit expansion, and external borrowing has led to macroeconomic imbalances which have acquired cancerous proportions in many market-economy countries.

The problem that the welfare state now faces is how to remove the imbalances that it has created. There being no agreed filter mechanism and motivating system other than prices and self-interest with the help of which to reduce aggregate demand, there is a call for placing primary reliance on the market and reducing the role of the state. While both of these are undoubtedly necessary, their use within the secular framework of value-neutrality tends to reduce, not the spending that benefits the vested interests, but rather the spending that hurts the objectives of both growth and equity.

This leads one to the conclusion that if the welfare state tries to pursue growth and equity within the framework of Pareto optimality, it will automatically get itself entangled in difficult macroeconomic imbalances. These will force it to roll back its frontiers. However, if it wishes to raise growth and equity without imbalances, it must offset increased spending on heads that contribute to these goals by a reduction in spending on heads that do not. Such discrimination requires value judgements based on a socially-agreed filter and an effective motivating system that could ensure the needed socio-economic restructuring. This is not possible in a secular framework.

INEQUITY OF THE SOCIALIST STRATEGY

The inequities of *laissez-faire* capitalism gave rise not only to the welfare state but also to socialism. Even though socialism proposed a different strategy, it was based on the same world-view as the market system; it was equally, if not more, secular in its outlook on life. However, in sharp contrast with the market system, it had an implicit distrust in the ability of human beings to act in the interest of society. It, therefore, relied primarily on the curbing of individual freedom and the profit motive and on the elimination of private property. Accordingly, state ownership of all means of production and central planning became the primary instruments of its strategy for promoting efficiency and equity in resource use.

The removal of profit as a direct reward for individual effort, however, erodes initiative and efficiency both of which are indispensable for growth. Centralised decision-making also makes the transfer of resources from one use to another slow and cumbersome and makes the whole economic machinery inefficient. Moreover, it was not realised that if individual human beings cannot be trusted to manage their private businesses within the overall constraint of social well-being, how can they manage the means of production of the whole nation for this purpose? Will the government officials not be from the same people who cannot be trusted? If so, what is the guarantee that they will not exploit the tremendous power exercised by them as the controllers of all means of production? What will motivate them to act in the interest of society? Even the central planning officials need a filter mechanism of prices and values and proper motivation to manage the means of production for actualising both efficiency and equity. Who will provide these? If they themselves try to set all prices and values, will there not be arbitrariness in their decisions and a conflict of interest, particularly in a system which has dialectics (the counterpart of social Darwinism) as an essential part of its world-view? Who will check them and correct them if necessary?

Socialism thus failed to provide an effective filter mechanism and motivating system for allocation and distribution of resources. Its triggering mechanism for the transfer of resources from one use to another was also slow and ineffective. This has been clearly borne out by facts. The record of socialism is much worse than that of the market system. It has failed in all countries where it was enforced. It could not fulfil needs or substantially reduce socio-economic inequalities in spite of the enormous resources of the countries which adopted it. Moreover, the socialist economies stagnated due to lack of motivation among workers as well as executives and the inability of the system to respond to changing realities. The external debt of these countries also rose steeply and is set to rise further at a rapid rate. Their effort to solve the problems, that socialism has got them into, by the adoption of market solutions, without discarding the diehard secularism of their world-view, is bound to accentuate the prevailing inequities and to engulf them in a host of economic problems, including inflation, unemployment and external debt, even more serious than what many market economy countries are experiencing. Unfortunately, the one thing that is conspicuously missing from all reorganisation programmes suggested by both the socialist and the free market circles for the reform of the socialist economies is the injection of a moral dimension into economic reform to ensure that the condition of the poor improves instead of becoming worse.

LESSON FOR DEVELOPING COUNTRIES

Both the systems have thus failed to realise their professed goals of need-fulfilment, full employment, and equitable distribution of income and wealth. This is because their world-view, and the strategy derived from it, are not in harmony with their professed goals. The goals are humanitarian, based on their religious ideals of justice, brotherhood and sacrifice for the good of others. The strategies are, however, based on the concepts of 'survival of the fittest' and 'maximum want satisfaction' in the market system, and 'class struggle' and 'material conditions of life' in socialism. Within the frame of reference of their world-views and strategies, these systems are unable to introduce the radical structural changes that are needed to realise growth with justice and stability. The inevitable conclusion of this discussion is that systems which have themselves failed to realise growth with justice and stability cannot serve as examples for developing countries, and particularly so for Muslim countries because of the unequivocal commitment of Islam to socio-economic justice.

THREE

INCONSISTENCY OF DEVELOPMENT ECONOMICS

In spite of the inability of both the market system and socialism to realise development with justice, all Muslim countries have been pursuing policies prescribed by development economics, which is an offshoot of both these systems and has, hence, the same world-view. It is, in fact, even worse because while the market and the sociolist economy countries have consistently pursued a single strategy with modifications over the years in the light of their experience, the allegiance of countries following the prescriptions of development economics has wavered between the two mutually conflicting strategies of these systems. The reason for this wavering allegiance is that development economics itself has so far passed through three different phases.[1]

The first of these three phases was the old growth economics of classical economists who tried to explain the long-run growth of the economy within the liberal framework of *laissez-faire* capitalism. This growth economics remained a leading concern of classical economists for less than a century after the publication of Adam Smith's *Wealth of Nations* in 1776. Thereafter it went into the background and the centre of classical economists' attention shifted to other areas of economics. Growth economics regained its importance in the second phase of development economics, which began after the Second World War when a number of the 'Third World' countries became independent and the analysis of problems relating to their development began to attract attention. However, *laissez-faire* capitalism had lost ground by that time as a result of the Great Depression and the problems of post-War reconstruction; and Keynesian economics and socialism had become popular.

In the second phase of development economics the focus shifted away from the liberalism of classical and neo-classical economics. It preached a lesser reliance on the market and a greater role for the government in the economy. But when the hold of Keynesian and socialist strategies began to weaken in the West in the 1970s and there was a resurgence of liberalism and neo-classical economics, development economics entered its third phase with another shift of focus. It became increasingly more anti-dirigiste and pro-free market. As a result, many of the problems now faced by developing countries are being blamed on the dominant role of the state in the economies and increased public sector spending over the three decades of the fifties, sixties and seventies, whether it be the inefficient use of scarce resources, the unduly large macroeconomic and external imbalances, the rising inequalities of income and wealth, or the social tensions.

This wavering allegiance of development economics, from the market to the state and back again to the market, has deprived it of a firm focus. It has led to conflicting analyses and policy prescriptions, and generated inconsistencies and uncertainties in the development programmes of developing countries, causing immense harm to the health and development of their economies. The task that these countries now face is doubly difficult. They have not only to develop their economies in a way that would lead to greater efficiency and equity in the use of their extremely scarce resources but also to remove the imbalances that false prescriptions have generated.

The question arises whether the new policies being prescribed in the light of neo-classical economics will help realise equity along with efficiency and stabilisation. To answer this question, it would be appropriate to see the impact that the Western world-view has had on development economics and the problems that it has generated for the developing countries.

Since neo-classical, Keynesian, and socialist economics all have their origin in the Enlightenment world-view, they are secular in their approach to the analysis of human problems and the realisation of human well-being. They place too much emphasis on consumption and material possessions as a source of human happiness and are not inwardly committed to human brotherhood and socio-economic justice. They disregard the role of moral values in the allocation and distribution of resources, and hence in development with justice and stability, and over-emphasise the role of the market or the state. Their strictly this-worldly perspective does not provide a rationale for anything other than materialism and social Darwinism. Within this framework there is no motivation to serve the social interest except where it is automatically served as an indirect result of serving the self-interest.

PESSIMISTIC OUTLOOK

The social-Darwinist approach of development economists along with their ethnocentricity led them to the introduction of a grain of pessimism in the development literature. The poverty, underdevelopment and political subjugation of poor countries, which happened to be primarily non-European and non-white, began to be ascribed to the cultural, racial and even mental inferiority of their peoples.[2] It was argued that these countries did not fulfil the preconditions that development required. Their values and social behaviour patterns were considered *a priori* to be inimical to the creation of these preconditions.

The most brazen expression of these views was made by Eugene Staley who said that the development of poor countries could be successful only if carried out in the image of the United States.[3] Even Myrdal, a relatively less ethnocentric Western economist, believed that the "modernisation ideals", which were necessary for development, were "alien" to these countries.[4] The United Nations and the World Bank, which were expected to be free from an ethnocentric bias, did not fulfil the expectation.[5]

The dominant view thus was that the developing countries would not be able to advance unless they 'modernised' themselves. Modernisation did not, however, consist in adopting better technology; it consisted rather in adopting Western materialist values and social institutions. These alone would motivate the people to work harder, to earn, save and invest more, and to adopt modern technology.

This undue emphasis on the lack of prerequisites for growth conceived within the image of Western culture led to the widespread acceptance of the "vicious circle of poverty" in the development literature. It was argued that developing countries would not be able to overcome the vicious circle of overpopulation, lower incomes, lower savings, lower investment, lower exports and lower growth that the lack of "modernisation ideals" created. They would hence be condemned to what Nurkse described as, a "low-level equilibrium that perpetuates itself".[6] Even the savings that they did realise by squeezing consumption could not be translated into capital goods because of their inability to raise their exports and foreign exchange earnings. These countries would not find it possible to overcome the two gaps — saving-investment and import-export — that they faced, and would not therefore be able to extricate themselves from the poverty trap.

Most of the development literature was thus imbued with a sense of deep pessimism about the prospects for growth in the developing countries.[7] Since patterns of living and values of life other than those of the enlightened West were considered *a priori* inimical to growth, little thought was given to the formulation of a development strategy that would be consistent with the resource endowment and values of the poorer countries. Williamson rightly admitted this in the early 1950s by saying:

> Economists generally have been too much concerned with static models and too culturally bound by a Western European framework of institutions to make the contribution to the subject of the economics of growth that might reasonably be expected from the profession.[8]

Experience has, however, clearly demonstrated that this pessimism concerning the prospects for development was seriously in error and that substantial growth has taken place in spite of widely varying initial endowments and circumstances. What continues to be a problem, however, is that because of policies framed and pursued within the perspective of value-neutrality, poverty has persisted and "the fruit of growth is concentrated in a few hands" in spite of growth.[9] In addition, the developing countries have become engulfed in macroeconomic imbalances and external debt of immense proportions. Why this is so will become clear in the following discussion.

The air of pessimism in the early years of development economics gave rise to the idea of a 'critical minimum effort'. In the absence of such effort, attempts to develop will fail.[10] But how could this critical minimum effort be mustered when the people were culturally backward and the savings and private initiative needed for this purpose were not available? The discussion led to the formulation of two divergent standpoints. One of these favoured adoption of the socialist strategy of a dominant role for the government in the economy through comprehensive planning, controls, and public enterprises, in sharp contrast with the extreme neo-classical view of relying primarily on the private sector and the market.[11] The other consisted of playing down the goal of socio-economic justice for developing countries.

DOMINANT GOVERNMENT ROLE

The *volte-face* in favour of a dominant role for the government in development literature was brought about by the initial success of totalitarian regimes in the USSR and China, and of Keynesian economics in the West. It began to be argued that the neo-classical economic model with its emphasis on markets and marginal economic adjustments in response to price changes was highly unrealistic for developing countries that were suffering from various cultural and structural rigidities.[12] The governments of developing countries should 'push' for development as hard as they could by playing a leading role in the economy. Only such a 'big push' could help them attain 'self-generating' or 'self-sustained' growth and the 'great leap forward'.[13]

The big push was to be attained by a wave of investments in a number of large-scale, capital-intensive industries. The theory of the big push thus had a built-in bias in favour of industry as against agriculture. Concentration on large-scale heavy industry and capital-intensive techniques was considered to be the only way by which a developing country could attain accelerated development.[14] Since the minimum economic size of a number of large-scale industrial projects required large investments, it was assumed that private entrepreneurs would be neither willing nor able to make such investments; such projects would hence have to be in the public sector.

The outcome of the 'big push' theory was an undue emphasis on the role of the public sector in economic growth. Neo-classical economics thus went into disrepute. It was replaced by the 'new' economics which placed greater emphasis on planning and government intervention, industrialisation, import-substitution, urban development and a host of other policies that led to a continually widening role for the government in the economy. Development economics generally acquired "a strong *dirigiste*, anti-free market, anti-capitalist bias".[15]

Comprehensive planning became increasingly important in country after country. Most of these plans called for the government to make virtually all major investments and to operate all capital goods industries. Many of these plans also called for a wide range of director controls. Planning was thus intended not just to provide guidance and a framework for development to maximise efficiency and equity, but was rather directed to the actual carrying out of investment projects by the government through public enterprises and the levying of direct controls.

NEGLECT OF EQUITY

The other impact of the air of pessimism was the belief that the goals of economic growth and socio-economic justice were incompatible and that, if the goal of accelerated growth was to be attained, the goal of equitable distribution must be compromised.[16]   This could not, however, be stated openly in development plans because of its adverse political implications. Hence, the plans continued to pay lip service to the goal of socio-economic justice by mentioning it among the objectives of planning. Effective measures were, however, not taken in most developing countries to make the goal of socio-economic justice a reality.

The anti-equity tone in development literature was in a way set in 1955 for almost a decade and a half by Sir Arthur Lewis, who wrote: "First it should be noted that our subject matter is growth and not distribution".[17] Bauer and Yamey argued in 1957 that "redistribution of income in favour of the poor is not likely to promote economic growth in the sense of greater output per head".[18] Even the United Nations ruled out distribution as a goal of policy by stating that "the most general objective of economic development is to maximise the national income or the rate of economic growth".[19] Professor Harry Johnson, writing in 1962, emphasised that it would be "unwise for a country anxious to enjoy rapid growth to insist too strongly on policies aimed at ensuring economic equality and a just income distribution".[20] Proverty, inequality and income distribution were virtually absent from consideration in the first edition of the widely used book of readings by Gerald Meier, *Leading Issues in Economic Development*, published in 1964. Even a conference of leaders in the field of economic development held in the mid-1960s made hardly any mention of the goals of reducing poverty and inequality, as is evident from the proceedings published in 1966.[21]

Some advocates of accelerated growth went to the extent of arguing in favour of "greater inequality of incomes on the grounds that the beneficiaries are likely to save a larger part of the income transferred to them and so add to capital formation".[22]   Misleading empirical support for such views was sought in the inverted-U curve, which has become associated with the name of Kuznets, even though it received little empirical support from Kuznets' own writings or from subsequent data. The Kuznets' curve was taken to imply that inequality is bound to increase in the early stages of development and will decrease only in the later stages. No consideration was given to the possibility that the Kuznets' curve may be the result of the economic system and the policies pursued, and might not necessarily reflect an iron law of nature.[23]

One of the most favoured explanations advanced for the rise in saving rate across industrial revolutions has been the rising inequality. Ever since Adam Smith, economic historians have stressed the growth-inequality trade-off, which is central to the classical labour-surplus model considered to be *a priori* true for all Third World countries. The evidence, however, has not been kind to the trade-off thesis. Rising inequality has accounted for little of America's or of Britain's saving experience. It appears to have made little contribution to contemporary savings.[24]

Even a policy of inflation was espoused because it lightens the repayment burden of the public exchequer and also 'forces' the public to save. It was argued that inflation has the ability to "bring about a redistribution in favour of individuals and classes who are likely to save a larger part of the income transferred".[25] Professor Lewis also argued eloquently that price rises resulting from 'mild' inflation serve to increase the profits of the industrial and mercantile classes, and by so doing, increase their savings, which are invested.[26] This reasoning was based on the false assumption that every penny paid in wages is spent on consumption and that every penny not paid to labour is necessarily saved and invested productively.

This trend of thought had its influence on leaders and policy-makers in developing countries. Even Jawaharlal Nehru, apparently a staunch believer in socio-economic justice, justified the trend towards increasing economic inequality in India by saying: "To some extent that is inevitable in a growing economy".[27] Some Muslim economists also joined the bandwagon, in spite of the clear and unequivocal emphasis of Islam on socio-economic justice, and projected the secularist, social-Darwinist view that indulgence in the goal of socio-economic justice was a luxury that only developed countries could afford. Dr Mahboobul Haq, who later became the Minister of Finance and Planning in Pakistan, wrote:

> The underdeveloped countries must consciously accept a philosophy of growth, and shelve for the distant future all ideas of equitable distribution and welfare state. It should be recognized that these are luxuries which only developed countries can afford.[28]

It was probably not realised that within the Islamic value frame it is inexcusable for a Muslim to commit, propagate or even condone injustice.

The socialist tendency in development economics therefore did not reflect the concern for equity that it did in Western and socialist countries. It reflected only the desire to accelerate growth through the use of planning and the coercive power of the state, with an even greater commitment to social Darwinism than was true for neo-classical economics. Socialism in the developing countries was "thus of a third type, different form that of the Communist countries as well as that of the Western world".[29] All that socialism really connoted in the Third World was a "commitment to nationalisation, and more generally, to state ownership and management of a large sector of the economy".[30] Socialism thus became "merely equated with planning".[31]

Even though there were a number of economists who continued to be concerned about equity even during this period, they were in the minority. The prevailing view was that the 'trickle-down' mechanism would ultimately solve the poverty and income distribution problems if only growth were fast enough.[32] The trickle-down mechanism, however, proved to be highly in-effective. This was bound to be the case. Poverty and income inequality are so sticky and pervasive that it was highly unrealistic to expect that they could be removed without making major structural changes in the economy and the financial system, and without creating values and a motivating system that would be conducive to their removal.

STERILE CONTROVERSIES

The lack of commitment on the part of development economics to a filter of socially-agreed values, and particularly to socio-economic justice, made it difficult to resolve the several hair-splitting controversies which have plagued it over the last three decades. The twin pillars of materialism and inequality on which development economics was founded could not provide a filter mechanism that could help resolve these controversies on different issues of social importance. The whims and personal preferences of the discussants, without any agreed criteria to guide them, led the discussion into an endless circular path. This was clearly the case irrespective of which controversy we look at: agriculture versus industrialisation, rural versus urban development, balanced versus unbalanced growth, import-substitution versus export promotion, and market forces versus planning.

Looked at from the point of view of realising the twin goals of efficiency and equity, the controversy appears to be sterile and unproductive. It reflects the absence of a focus — the focus of socio-economic justice as a goal for development. It also indicates a lack of awareness of the different phases in which developing countries are, the diversity of their socio-economic circumstances, the complexities of human society, and the factors which motivate human beings to work for their self-interest without crossing the bounds of social interest. The harm that the controversy has done is reflected in the bottlenecks, imbalances, slow growth rates, higher inflation, burdensome debt and social unrest that most developing countries are now facing. Had a filter mechanism of agreed values been available and socio-economic justice had been a clear target of policies, the strategy for development would not have been involved in as much controversy as the development literature has witnessed.

AGRICULTURE VERSUS INDUSTRY

Since a majority of the population in developing countries lives in rural areas, its well-being could only have been ensured through rural and agricultural development. Rural development was, therefore, not an option. It was indispensable. Rural development could not, however, have taken place without support from industrial development. To enable the farmers to undertake investments in fertilisers, better seeds and improved technology, it was necessary to raise their incomes. This was not possible without providing employment to the unemployed and the underemployed members of rural families. It would not be possible to do so without simultaneously developing small-scale and micro industries in rural areas.

Thus, for a great majority of developing countries, industrialisation, like agricultural development, was also not an option. It had to be a fundamental part of the policy objectives. It was necessary to attain balanced development if the objective was to expand employment opportunities, satisfy the basic needs of the entire population, and reduce inequalities. Neither agriculture nor industrialisation could by itself help developing countries realise such development. Diversification and modernisation of all sectors of their economies was necessary.

Agricultural and industrial development were, therefore, not the alternatives to choose from. They were rather complementary and mutually supporting with respect to both input and output. The issue was not industrial or agricultural development but rather the human being and his well-being. Had the well-being of all been the goal, the interrelationship between industry and agriculture and the contribution that each can make to the other and to the realisation of agreed socio-economic goals would have been appreciated.

Within this context any development programme that propounds unbalanced growth and overemphasises industrialisation relative to agriculture, or agriculture relative to industry, could not but lead to injustice and misery and also create a bottleneck, which it would be difficult to remove without a reversal of policies to restore a balance. Such reversals are normally difficult and traumatic.

Import-Substitution versus Export Promotion

If industry and agriculture are both to be developed, then the strategic importance of both import-substitution and export promotion in the socio-economic advancement of developing countries needs to be clearly visualised. There is no reason to emphasise one to the exclusion of the other. Both are necessary, even though their importance may vary over a longer time horizon corresponding to the different phases in the country's development.

This does not mean that import-substitution should be undertaken at any cost.[33] Since the ultimate goal is the efficient and equitable use of scarce resources to realise general well-being, all tariff and non-tariff barriers must be weighed against the realisation of socio-economic justice and the promotion of economic development. The rational principles of resource allocation cannot, therefore, be lost sight of; the cost of economic inefficiency will be reflected in the non-realisation of goals and will ultimately have to be borne by the people. This cannot be justified. Nevertheless, import-substitution at all cost became an anchor of policy in many developing countries because it satisfied the vested interest of the rich and the powerful. The slogan of reducing external dependence was used to appeal to the national sentiment of the masses.

It was therefore not the policy of import-substitution *per se* which was wrong; it was rather the way in which this policy was implemented. If equity had been one of the primary goals of development, the policy of import-substitution would have been used initially to support primarily agriculture and small and micro enterprises (SMEs) in developing countries. This would have helped fulfil needs and expand employment opportunities in rural areas and small towns. Workers would have found jobs either in their own villages and towns or near them. They would have thus not been uprooted from their families and social surroundings.

What was done instead was the promotion of large-scale industries in urban centres through full government support in the form of subsidised inputs, overvalued exchange rates, and unduly high tariffs on competing imports. International support was also available mainly for such industries. Large projects were "eye-catchers and even international agencies tend to prefer large-scale projects".[34]

Agriculture and SMEs suffered from lack of any subsidy or protection and from overvalued official exchange rates. Techniques remained antiquated, productivity low, and income, savings and investment could not rise significantly. Unemployment and underemployment rose. Import-substituting large-scale industries prospered because of the low cost of their capital and inputs and the protection they received through high tariff walls and overvalued exchange rates. Moreover, since equity and need-fulfilment were not the primary goals of economic policy, even the selection of import-substituting industries did not take this into consideration.

If this had been done, there would have been a positive advance in the direction of need-fulfilment, although the employment goal would still have suffered. Many of the import-substituting large-scale industries were not related to needs; they were rather related to luxuries, consumer durable and heavy capital goods — industries in which a need-oriented development programme would not have taken a serious interest in the initial phase of development. Such industries also became constrained by the size of the domestic market. Being inefficient, they could not compete in the export market. They nevertheless led to an increase in the volume of imports, particularly in the case of industries which had to import not only capital goods but also raw materials. The imports they needed could not be cut back. Hence what many of them accomplished in reality was to substitute one kind of imports for another.

The growth of large-scale import-substituting industries, many of which depended on imported capital goods and raw materials, did not increase significantly the demand for the output of agriculture and SMEs. The 'linkage' effect did not therefore take place. The benefit mostly leaked abroad through a rise in induced imports. Moreover, the technologies adopted in these industries were predominantly capital-intensive, being designed for countries that have abundance of capital and scarcity of labour.[35] Employment directly generated by expansion of these industries was, therefore, relatively small.

Even a substantial part of the meagre domestic savings came to be diverted into these industries at lower or subsidised rates of interest compared with what prevails in the rural areas. The proportion of savings going into agriculture and SMEs was thus small — not necessarily because of lack of savings in those sectors but rather because of the misallocation of savings. The unduly large support given to large-scale industries, therefore, ruined handicraft industries, particularly handlooms. The bulk of the rural population had no choice but to remain underemployed in rural areas or to migrate to the overcrowded urban centres.

This is not an argument against large-scale capital-intensive industries *per se*, which do have a place in development. However, since expansion of self-employment and employment opportunities enjoys priority, large-scale capital-intensive industries should get the green light only when they are indispensable and the job that they can do cannot be done effectively by labour intensive SMEs.

The particular trend that import-substitution took was natural, given the propagation of Western life-styles, the lack of an indigenous development philosophy, and the absence of a motivating system to induce people successfully to abstain from unnecessary and conspicuous consumption. This was exacerbated by the vested interest of Western manufacturers of capital goods and raw materials in the production of goods for conspicuous consumption. They did effective salesmanship and also arranged financing through suppliers' credits and loans from banks and official lending institutions. Imports therefore rose without a corresponding rise in exports and foreign exchange bottlenecks became more acute.

However, if the policy of industrialisation and import substitution had been pursued to promote equity, an entirely different approach could have been adopted. The primary objective would have been to fulfil needs, enlarge employment opportunities, and reduce inequalities rather than to serve the interests of foreign exporters and rich domestic investors. Everything would have been done to encourage and help rural and urban entrepreneurs to produce the needed consumer and capital goods for the domestic market and for export. The help would have included not only tariff protection but also the creation of an efficient physical, social and financial infrastructure in rural areas in addition to import or domestic development of simple but efficient technology for the SMEs. This would have enabled them to increase production and also, ultimately, to compete effectively with foreign goods. Employment and income would have risen in rural areas, with less congestion in urban centres. The rising incomes of the rural population would also have helped agriculture by enabling the farmers to use better agricultural inputs.

Import-substitution policy implemented within this framework would have enabled the SMEs initially to meet the domestic demand and ultimately to export. Exports do not necessarily have to be goods which are not also in demand in the domestic market. Production can be for both the domestic and the foreign markets. In the first stage, however, production can be for the domestic market, and later on, when capacity has increased and the external economies have been realised, the fruits of the export market can also be reaped.

Such a policy would have helped developing countries utilise their advantage in the production and export of simple, need-fulfilling goods and services and the capital goods related to these. This course of initial industrialisation does not imply that at a later stage of development, when needs have been largely fulfilled and the unemployment problem has been solved, import-substitution and export promotion in the field of consumer-durable and heavy capital goods cannot become a target of national policy.

While import-substitution did not take the right course, export promotion did not take place either. Many of the capital intensive industries that were established did not have a comparative advantage in the initial phase of development and, in spite of overt and covert subsidies, they could not compete in the export market. Agriculture and labour-intensive small-scale industries, which could have been made to have a comparative advantage, did not get the needed official support and credit to expand their output. The overvalued exchange rate also hurt them and they could not compete effectively in the export market. Exports therefore did not rise as much as they could have.

The recent reversal of emphasis on export promotion needs to be considered with caution.[36] If import-substitution at all costs is bad, export promotion at all costs is also not desirable. The ultimate impact of any policy on socio-economic justice must never be lost sight of, given the fact that a number of inefficient large-scale industries have been established. A heavy dose of devaluation of the local currency along with freezing of nominal wages (two of the crutches on which the export strategy stands) may enable the inefficient urban industries established by the rich and the influential to export and thus survive, but would hurt the poor by substantially lowering their real wages. It would be at variance with the objective of socio-economic justice. Thus, before jumping on to the bandwagon of export promotion, all necessary measures should be taken to ensure that the benefit goes to the poor rather than the rich.

Those who over-emphasise the strategy of export promotion to the neglect of import-substitution, should also bear in mind that the exports of developing countries have always faced and continue to face all kinds of tariff and non-tariff barriers in industrial countries and that their imports have been influenced by dumping and predatory pricing by industrial countries. Government aid to agriculture and industry has grown substantially in the industrial countries over the last three decades and barriers against imports have proliferated.

These support programmes and protectionist measures have affected mainly the imports of developing countries. For example, virtually no rice imports are permitted in Japan and the domestically produced rice is sold at about nine times the world price, despite recent reductions in support prices.[37] While tariffs have been steadily reduced, protection via non-tariff barriers involves major trade, employment and welfare costs for developing countries.[38] Moreover, any developing country that tries hard and manages to become a big exporter soon faces iron walls of quota ceilings imposed by industrial countries, thus finding it difficult to expand its exports further. UNCTAD has estimated the total economic cost of protectionist barriers against Third World countries to be as high as $700 billion annually in terms of export earnings — more than fifty percent of the total current external debt of these countries.[39]

UNANTICIPATED PROBLEMS

While the pundits of development economics emphasised a substantially large government role to overcome the prevailing pessimism about the prospects for growth, they did not give any serious thought to the development of a strategy for making an offsetting reduction in claims on resources elsewhere. Wholesale adoption of Western consumer culture was in fact propagated, and even countries in their initial stages of development were pushed into the high living and gadgetry of Rostow's fifth stage. Arms build-up was also promoted with concessionary financing. This raised the import of luxury goods and military hardware and unwarrantably widened the import-export gap. It also lowered the propensity to save and made the internally generated savings inadequate to satisfy the rising need for investment. Hence, the savings-investment gap also widened. Squeezing the wasteful and inessential absorption would have required value judgement, which the value-free development economics could not entertain. Within its instrument-kit, taxes and inflation were the main tools available for squeezing consumption.

However, tax revenues could not be raised in step with spending because of the narrow tax base and inefficient and corrupt tax administration in developing countries. Budgetary and current account deficits thus rose steeply. To finance these deficits, Keynesian economics encouraged monetary expansion and the 'two-gap' approach pointed towards foreign aid.[40] Those who encouraged monetary expansion probably did not realise that developing countries, with their structural bottlenecks and supply constraints, were prone to a higher rate of inflation and greater import-export gap than the developed industrial countries.

Those who emphasised aid probably did not realise that only a very small portion of aid takes the form of grants; most of it is usually in the form of loans, which must be repaid with interest. Monetary expansion and heavy borrowing (both internal and external) thus became the crutches on which governments heavily relied. Once the governments had become dependent on these, it was difficult to reverse the steps; a deep cut in spending or a steep rise in taxes, which the reversal demands, have always been politically unpopular.

INFLATION

Infltion became rampant, but this was also initially justified.[41]   The Phillips curve provided policy makers with the needed rationale in the form of a trade-off between inflation on the one hand, and higher growth and employment on the other.   Most Keynesian economists felt little concern about inflation and continued to urge expansionary policies throughout the post-World War II period.[42]   Professor Henry Bruton, in a series of lectures delivered at the University of Bombay in 1961, said that "a case could be made for making inflation an instrument of policy, rather than the control of inflation an objective of policy".[43]   Warnings were, no doubt, usually added against monetary mismanagement by saying that "a naive note printing extravaganza does nothing but harm".[44]

Such warnings, however, were usually not taken seriously by planners and finance ministers in most developing countries.   Inflation offered a way of 'covert taxation without consent'.   Unlike the higher taxes, it did not immediately raise the political uproar and was thus an easy way of financing the burgeoning deficits.   If there were any unpleasant consequences, it would be their successors and not they themselves, who would have to face them. Such behaviour should have been expected as the most natural in a system in which socio-economic justice is not a fundamental goal, and the pursuit of self-interest is the primary objective of life.   There was no reason to expect that bureaucrats and political leaders would act differently in a value-free environment.

Inflation tended to redistribute income upward, thus tilting the balance against the goal of socio-economic justice.   This alone would probably not have given development economists pause for thought.   There were, however, other adverse effects which have affected development adversely and will continue to do so for quite some time in the future.

Inflation led to price controls and subsidies on foodgrains and other essential items of consumption.   While price controls hurt the growth in long-term supply of these goods, subsidies loaded the government budgets with a heavy burden which the governments now find it difficult to bear.   Inflation also led to overvalued exchange rates which were adopted by governments to hold down inflationary pressures.

This encouraged imports and hurt exports by making them uncompetitive in the international market. Agriculture and SMEs were particularly hard hit because they did not get the support that large-scale industries received. The dependence on imports increased and the foreign exchange deficit rose further. This raised the need for borrowing and exacerbated the debt-servicing burden. Even though the governments would now like, under the IMF and World Bank pressure, to remove price controls and subsidies, and to adopt realistic exchange rates, they find it politically difficult to do so because of adverse impact on cost of living. Sir Arthur Lewis was thus led to exclaim: "The principal lesson we have all learned, less-developed countries and more-developed countries alike, is that inflation is a scourge."[45]

DEBT BURDEN

As a result of heavy doses of borrowing, both internal and external debts of developing countries have risen steeply.[46] This was at first justified serenely. But now, the internal and external imbalances faced by developing countries have become so serious that they have created a nightmare for all those concerned with development policies and the health of the domestic as well as international financial systems. The use of shallow domestic financial markets for large government borrowing not only crowded out the private sector but also made financial institutions weak; loaded down with low-yield government debt, they were unable to provide for adequate reserves against losses through bad debts. The heavy resort to multinational banks for external borrowing, initially justified on the basis of the supposed insolvency of sovereign debtors, has raised the debt burden to such an unbearable level that the inability of debtor countries to service the debt is threatening the very survival of these banks. Even the developmental process has now become jeopardised. Real rates of growth have slowed down. Efforts to reduce inflation and the external imbalance may slow it down even further.

PLANNING DIFFICULTIES

While the problems of excessive government spending were not anticipated, even the difficulties of comprehensive planning were underestimated and the expected results overestimated. The ability to formulate development plans was severely limited by the lack of requisite data and the imperfect character of such statistics as are available. Efforts tended to be large because the data were inadequate to calculate such strategic variables as total saving, capital coefficients, the extent of underemployment, or the value of an investment project.

Moreover, there was a tendency to expect too much from a planning model. It was not realised that a planning model could not remove or simplify the hard choices that policy makers had to make. Conflicts among multiple objectives that were frequently encountered in development programmes could not be resolved without establishing priorities. An econometric model could not take the place of a development philosophy which provides guidelines in terms of agreed goals and values, that cannot be established within the framework of Pareto optimality. A development philosophy and motivation on the part of policy makers and the public were needed to take and accept decisions ungrudgingly in the larger interest of general well-being. The absence of such a philosophy and motivating system explains why almost all development plans placed equity among the goals of planning but none of them laid down an effective programme to realise it.

Problems of implementing the comprehensive plans were also not given adequate attention. Many development plans met on paper the tests of efficiency and consistency (though not equity), but failed in practice due, in large measure, to deficiencies in political and administrative requirements. The implementation of plans tended to be extremely difficult because their formulation had been based on the most advanced econometric models. The plans were too refined for practical implementation. Most developing countries could have benefited "more from sound application of fundamental elementary principles of economics than from attempts to use the highest style theory".[47]

The macroeconomic models had a built-in preference in favour of the quantifiable to the relative neglect of components that are not quantifiable but are of crucial importance for realising the plan objectives, particularly socio-economic justice. The more rigorous an econometric model, the less was it likely to incorporate non-economic components. As Professor Galbraith observed: "On even the most preliminary view of the problem, effective government, education, and social justice emerge as critically important. In many countries, in diagnosing the barriers to advancement, it is lack of these that is of critical importance. And it follows that until these barriers are removed little will come from capital investment and technical assistance. While plans will be big on paper they will be small in result."[48]

RESURGENCE OF NEO-CLASSICAL ECONOMICS

The difficulties now faced by developing countries have led to a resurgence of neo-classical economics. The blame is being laid squarely on the socialist strategy of big government and comprehensive planning followed over a period of about three decades. It is being argued that heavy reliance on public sector investments and controls for promoting growth has led not only to distortions in resource allocation but also to macroeconomic and external imbalances. It has hindered full realisation of the initiative and investment potential of the private sector. The enthusiasm for large-scale capital-intensive heavy industries has led to inefficient industrialisation at the cost of rural and agricultural development. As Michael Camdessus, Managing Director of the IMF, has clearly emphasised:

> Economies that suffer from rampant inflation, large budget deficits, pervasive trade restrictions, misaligned exchange rates, unrealistic interest rates, heavy external debt and repeated bouts of capital flight cannot and do not grow rapidly for any sustained period of time.[49]

Even more disconcerting than the lagging growth and imbalances has been the failure of poor countries to alleviate the condition of the masses living in absolute poverty, the increasing number of the unemployment and underemployment, and the persistence of inequality. The problems faced by the poor have increased rather than decreased. The expectations, that independence and promises made by national governments had raised, have remained unfulfilled.

The resurgence of neo-classical economics in the wake of failure of the socialist strategy has thus brought the developing countries back to where they had started from the problem of realising both efficiency and equity in the use of scarce resources. Development economics, it must be admitted, has a different face this time around, at least so it appears. It is not concerned merely with growth, it is also concerned with equity.

This has been so since the beginning of the 1970s when it began to be recognised that development must mean not only growth in average per capita income but also a reduction in poverty.[50] It began to be realised that in the case of poor and heavily populated nations like India, Bangladesh, Pakistan, and Indonesia, only long-term, sustained, equitably distributed growth of per capita income offers the majority of people any hope of economic advancement. It simply may not be possible to "grow first and redistribute later."[51]

Development economics is, thus, no longer worshipping merely at the altar of GNP, praying for its growth only, it also claims to be a devotee of redistribution. The call is for "growth with redistribution", "reduction of absolute poverty", and "meeting basic human needs". Neo-classical economics does not now purport to be just the "guardian of rationality", it also wishes to be the "trustee of the poor".[52]

Addressing the World Bank's Annual Meeting in Nairobi in 1973, Robert McNamara, the then President of the Bank, called upon the world to focus on those in "absolute poverty" — those "who suffer a condition of life so degraded by disease, illiteracy, malnutrition, and squalor as to deny its victims basic human necessities".[53] Theodore Schultz, while accepting the Nobel Prize in 1979, stated:

> Most of the people in the world are poor, so if we knew the economics of being poor we would know much of the economics that really matters.[54]

Gerald Meier, from the first edition (1964) of whose *Leading Issues in Economic Development*, poverty, inequality and income distribution were virtually absent, led off the fourth edition (1984) with a substantial emphasis on income distribution in developing countries; and went even to the extent of saying that "emerging from poverty" is the "economics that really matters" (in another book of his, also published in 1984).[55] This concern for distribution is eloquently epitomised by Dudley Seers when he says:

> The questions to task about a country's development are therefore: what has been happening to poverty? What has been happening to unemployment? What has been happening to inequality? If all three of these have declined from high levels, then beyond doubt this has been a period of development for the country concerned. If one or two of these central problems have been growing worse, especially if all three have, it would be strange to call the result development even if per capita income doubled.[56]

THE CRUCIAL QUESTION

Thus we see that socio-economic justice, which had been declared to be an outcast in the interest of rapid capital formation and growth, has been readmitted as an objective. This is without doubt a welcome change. Development economics now gives at least the same outward appearance that neo-classical, Keynesian, and socialist economics have always given — aspiring to realise both equity and efficiency. However, the crucial question is whether the value-neutral neo-classical economics is capable of providing an effective strategy for realising both these goals in developing countries.

The strategy being currently emphasised by neo-classical economists in every paper and at every international or regional conference, is 'adjustment'. No one can challenge the need for adjustment. Given the severe imbalances faced by developing countries, adjustment is no longer an option, it has become a must. What is more important, however, is the components of an adjustment programme, and it is doubtful whether the components that neo-classical economics stands for can help realise both equity and efficiency.

Everyone will probably agree that the 'right' adjustment is that which addresses itself to both the demand and the supply sides of the problem in such a way that there is a 'minimum sacrifice of growth'. On the demand side, it is necessary to reduce domestic absorption, which refers to the aggregate of private and public consumption and investment outlays $(C+I+G)$. However, if future growth is to be ensured, then the reduction in absorption should be primarily in the consumption component of absorption and not in investment. Moreover, if socio-economic justice is also to be realised, then the decline in consumption needs to be brought about in such a way that the adverse effects fall on those who are better off and strong enough to bear the required austerity, and that the condition of the poor is at least not made worse, if it cannot, for some strong reason, be made better, which is the most desirable alternative. Socio-economic justice also demands that the rise in output be brought about in such a way that needs are fulfilled, employment rises and inequalities are reduced.

In contrast, the adjustment programme proposed by neo-classical economics, of which the World Bank and the IMF are the bastions, "will result", as Barber Conable, ex-President of the World Bank, had frankly admitted, "in some temporary unemployment, and in real difficult short-term reductions in living standards — which sometimes affect the poorest segment

of the population most harshly".[57] However, an economic system strongly
committed to socio-economic justice cannot permit the poorest segment of the
population to be affected "most harshly". The palliative that the harsh effect
may be "temporary" or "short-term" does not reduce the shock because the
likelihood is that this effect may not only be permanent but probably also
cumulative. Conable was, however, not wrong in his prediction about the
impact of adjustment on the poor. His prediction had been made within the
framework of neo-classical economics. It is, therefore, important to see why
the poor, who had been hit harshly by the secularist development economics
during the expansion phase, will be hit harshly once again by neo-classical
economics during the adjustment phase.

CONTENTS OF LIBERALISATION

The adjustment programme offered by neo-classical economics hangs
mainly by the thread of liberalisation. This call for liberalisation is couched
essentially in the value-neutral terms of Enlightenment philosophy. In spite
of a great deal of talk about economists being "trustees of the poor", there is
no commitment to a filter mechanism of socially-agreed values or to a
motivating system that could induce the rich and the powerful to absorb the
harsh effect of adjustment, and thus help ensure socio-economic justice. The
harsh effect on the poor is expected to be offset only indirectly — mainly by
creating an environment for higher growth through the restoration of internal
and external balance.

The most important components of neo-classical liberalisation, as
articulated by the IMF in its adjustment programmes, are: a) reduce the role
of government in the economy; b) allow the market to play its role; and c)
liberalise foreign trade. Stabilisation and efficiency, which are the main
targets, are to be attained by achieving "a sustainable external balance" and
by "restraining aggregate domestic demand, promoting supply, and, most
important, improving economic efficiency".

It has been honestly admitted that "distributional issues are primarily an
internal political concern."[58] Hence, "mitigation of the adverse distributional
implications of exogenous shocks or of the economic adjustments necessitated
by past, inappropriate policies has not been an explicit objective of Fund-
supported programmes", even though these adjustment programmes have
"important distributional implications."[59] Consequently, none of the IMF

annual consultation reports on member countries ever discusses a member country's progress in removing poverty, fulfilling needs, and reducing inequalities. A country gets full laurels from the IMF if it succeeds in reducing the imbalances irrespective of whether this has been attained with or without an adverse effect on equity.

It is argued that a reduced role for the government in the economy will help reduce domestic absorption by introducing fiscal restraint and cutting the budgetary deficit. The private sector will thus be able to play a greater and more active role in the economy and, being better motivated in its own self-interest, will contribute to greater efficiency. Restraints on credit expansion will help reduce private sector absorption. Greater reliance on the market will help in 'getting the prices right' (including interest rates and exchange rates) and in giving the 'right' signals to economic agents. This will remove distortions and lead to a more efficient allocation of resources.

While such a policy would lead to a rise in the prices of most goods and services in developing countries, the neo-classical prescription calls for a restraint on real wages. Although this will "impose hardship on organised labour,"[60] it will ultimately be offset by higher employment and growth. Outward orientation will help the adjusting country take advantage of international trade to promote growth and to offset the recessionary effect of reduction in domestic absorption. All import restrictions should be removed and imports and exports should both be encouraged. Realistic exchange rates will themselves go a long way in expanding exports and reducing imports, thus reducing the current account deficit. If tariffs have to be used, they should preferably be low and uniform. Any discrimination will require value judgements which are not desirable; it will only lead to distortions which will adversely affect efficiency. Import-substitution, it is argued, has only a limited potential because its target is basically the domestic market, which is limited, while exports do not face such a quantitative limitation.

While liberalisation calls for a cut in overall government spending, it does not address itself to a change in the composition of government spending to improve the equity performance of the budget. There is no discussion of ways of raising the quality and quantity of health, housing, transport, sanitation and educational facilities for the poor to uplift the quality of the human factor in development. Even a discussion of the supply side and Fund programmes is concerned primarily with providing better incentives to promote savings, investments, and exports through realistic prices, interest rates, exchange rates, and taxes. There is no discussion of economic restructuring to increase the supply of need-satisfying goods and services. 'Getting the prices right' through reliance on the market to give the 'right' signals to economic agents is thus the linchpin of the neo-classical prescription for solving the allocation and distribution problems of developing countries.

It has already been argued that the reliance on merely the price mechanism to allocate resources cannot but operate against need fulfilment and equitable distribution of income and wealth. This aspect of liberalisation is not expressly spelt out by neo-classical economists. It is, however, at the back of their minds when they make the stark prediction about the effect on the poor. They assume, and their assumption is realistic within their value-free framework, that nothing can be done to avoid the "most harsh" effect on the poor. Any effort to avoid the result of market forces will create distortions that will lead to inefficiency and lower growth. Accordingly, the only preferable alternative is to allow higher growth attained through liberalisation to improve the position of the poor.

However, the question is: will higher growth automatically lead to equity? If it could, the rich industrial countries would have long succeeded in eliminating poverty and reducing inequalities. This clearly shows that social Darwinism is unmistakenly present at the core of neo-classical economics even though outwardly it presents a smiling face to the poor — a wolf in sheep's clothing.

JUST DEVELOPMENT IN THE FAR EAST

Nevertheless, the neo-classical prescription is gaining momentum in developing countries. In its support are being cited the examples of Far Eastern countries like Japan, Taiwan, the Republic of Korea (South Korea), Hong Kong, and Singapore, which resorted to policies of liberalisation and export-orientation to promote efficiency and growth. It is argued that liberalisation helped accelerate their development by motivating their private sectors to greater initiative and efficiency. The outward-orientation enlarged their export surplus and increased not only employment opportunities in these countries but also enabled them to meet the foreign exchange needs of their expanding economies with less heavy reliance on foreign aid.

FACTORS RESPONSIBLE FOR JUST DEVELOPMENT

While there is no doubt that liberalisation and export-orientation have played a significant role in the accelerated growth of these countries, it is not correct to give the entire credit for their economic success to these two factors. There are several other factors which were equally, if not more, responsible. Some of these are: substantial government intervention, socio-economic justice and social harmony brought about by extensive land reforms and social values, high propensity to save and invest, and active support of import-substitution as well as export-promotion for industrialisation. Not all of these factors fit into the neo-classical model; in fact some of them are clearly in conflict with it.

Government Role

Governments in these countries have played, and continue to play, an important role. Only in the case of Hong Kong has anything close to *laissez-faire* been practised. In other countries there is extensive intervention in the form of state enterprise, subsidies, regulations and other measures affecting the capital market, domestic savings, trade, and almost every aspect of the economy. The governments have also directed private business into targeted channels through their control over industrial licences, foreign loans and technology agreements, and use of selective incentives and threats.[61] It is not possible to call Japan, South Korea, Taiwan, and Singapore liberal in the neo-classical sense.[62] With respect to Japan, Yasuo Masai says:

> Although the extent of direct state participation in economic activities is limited, the government's control and influence over business is stronger and more pervasive than in most other countries. This control is not exercised through legislation or administrative action but through constant — and to an outsider almost obsessive — consultation with business and through the authorities' deep indirect involvement in banking. . . . The need for large-scale government participation in economic activities is thereby obviated and, unlike many governments in the free-enterprise world, the state appears to be reluctant to extend its direct role.[63]

It is doubtful if these countries could have achieved as much as they did without an active and strong role of their governments.

It must, however, be admitted that the government role in these countries has not necessarily been restrictive in the form of controls that inhibit the initiative and drive of the private sector. It has rather been positive to facilitate and encourage the private sector. Of course, the pragmatic, growth-oriented and dedicated leadership of these countries has made possible the taking of right decisions in the interest of the country, and the stability of government has removed uncertainties about policies and inspired the confidence of investors.

Land Reforms and Wealth Distribution

Thoroughgoing land reforms were introduced in Japan, south Korea and Taiwan after the Second World War by the occupation authorities with the objective of destroying, psychologically and materially, the feudal lords who constituted the driving force behind these countries' war-effort. These reforms had the far-reaching side effects of equalising rural income distribution and keeping rural/urban differentials much narrower than in other countries.

In all three cases, land reforms were extensive. They destroyed the power base of feudal lords and virtually eliminated farm tenancy, which was widespread before the reforms. The land reforms reduced the average family holding in Japan to about 2.5 acres and in South Korea to about 2.25 acres of arable land.[64] The scale of landholding has remained unchanged to 1.2 hectares (2.9 acres) in Japan, with only 4 percent of all farms operating on land of more than 3 hectares (7.41 acres).[65] According to Sacks, land reforms in these countries "were probably more extensive than in any other case in modern history and could be accomplished because of the extraordinary national circumstances in each country" — Japan and South Korea were under U.S. occupation while Taiwan was under the Nationalists. The landlords in these countries could not therefore effectively mobilise political opposition.[66] The land reforms in essence also brought about a substantial expropriation of landlords because compensation was either not paid or was inadequate.

The redistributive effect of these land reforms was further reinforced by the destruction of wealth by war in all the three countries and the erosion in the real value of compensation received as well as of financial assets (bonds and cash holdings) by the high rate of inflation. In 1947 the annual inflation rates reached 334 percent in Japan, and in 1950 reached 500 percent in the

Republic of Korea, and 3400 percent in Taiwan in 1967. All these factors had the effect of substantially narrowing the gaps in income and wealth distribution. In the absence of this, liberalisation would have probably led to greater inequity.

The creation of a large body of small independent proprietary farmers in place of a tiny class of rich, unpopular landlords shifted the balance of political power in favour of the peasantry. The peasants could now assert their newly-gained political clout to tilt decisions in their own favour by the governments which needed their support and which thus became obliged to give protection to agriculture and to develop the rural infrastructure. The infrastructure, along with the transfer of land ownership, enabled the peasants to serve their interests and thus provided the necessary motivation to make improvements and long-term investments in agriculture. Given the small size of landholdings, the farmers successfully used simple, labour-intensive techniques (superior seeds, better methods of crop cultivation, and increased input of manure and fertilizers) to generate a substantial rise in output and incomes. This not only supplied the food needed by the rapidly growing population but also the savings and the market needed for industrial expansion.

What liberalisation did was that it enabled the *nouveaux riches* to become a dynamic element within the economy by making it possible for them to invest their savings in Western technology and machinery. This led to a rapid expansion in industrial output through the establishment of a large number of mutually competing manufacturing units. There was thus a simultaneous and balanced growth of both agriculture and industry. In the absence of liberalisation, the *nouveaux riches* may have been led into the unproductive fields of conspicuous consumption and capital flight, as has been the case in many developing countries.

Social Equality

The broad sharing of the benefits of growth that land reforms brought about ushered in greater social equality. This reduced conspicuous consumption and the related investments that income inequality usually promotes among the rich. It also released resources for the need fulfilment of the poor, thus improving their health and educational level. A well-fed, healthy and better-educated labour force established a firm foundation for faster and sustained growth. Reduction in the suffering of the poor removed anti-social feelings among them, improved their motivation for work and efficiency, and reduced the waste resulting from strikes and conflict. According to Sacks, economic success in Latin America has been impeded by social conflict over vast income inequalities, the distribution of income in Latin America being more unequal than in most other parts of the world. In Brazil the richest fifth have 33 times as much as the poorest fifth, whereas in Taiwan they have only a little over four times as much. On an average, the richest 20 percent are 21 times as rich in Latin America, but nine times as rich in East Asia.[68]

Labour-Intensive Techniques

Equity was further reinforced by the choice of labour-intensive policies which have helped the cause of employment in these countries. However, unlike Japan and South Korea, Taiwan also opted for an effective role by small enterprises in both agriculture and manufacturing, and did not allow the establishment of large conglomerates in domestic business.[69] This policy not only provided further support to the labour-intensive techniques in reducing unemployment and under-employment — a constant problem in other industrial and developing countries — but also provided small farmers good opportunities for rural earnings. This gave a boost to rural incomes; by 1980, almost three-quarters of the income of rural families came from non-agricultural income.[70]

Thus Taiwan was transformed over time from an economy having an abundance of labour in the 1950s to one having a scarcity of labour in the 1970s. The achievement of full employment in rural as well as urban areas led to a rise in the incomes of all families and further improved the level of income equality already attained as a result of land reforms.[71] As a consequence, the Gini Coefficient has continually declined in Taiwan from 0.56 in the 1950s to 0.31 in the early 1980s.[72] Taiwan has thus achieved a greater degree of income equality than any of the developing economies. the ratio of income of the richest 20 percent of the population to income of the poorest 20 percent declined from 20.5 in 1953 to 4.2 in 1980 and is probably the lowest ratio in the developing countries.[73]

Cultural Values

The cultural values of these countries and the homogeneity of population in most of them also helped promote the growth of a closely-knit society with social peace and stability. Their value system is centred on personal obligation — obligation to one's parents, employer and employees, friends and neighbours, and the community. These obligations need to be fulfilled in order for one to be accepted as a member of the society. If one were to refuse or neglect them, the inevitable consequence was social ostracisation. In a society where obligation occupies such an important position, group discipline is strong, the employer treats the employee humanely and pays due attention to his well-being, the employee works hard and conscientiously, and the employer/employee relations are congenial. This aspect of social values which keeps self-interest under check and serves social interest even when the two may not coincide, is certainly not in harmony with the value-free liberalisation of neo-classical economics.[74]

The perplexing question, however, is: Why did these cultural values remain dormant before the War? The answer is that such values require an enabling environment for their observance. Two factors created such an environment in post-War Japan. One of them was socio-economic equality which was brought about by post-War political and economic restructuring. In such an environment everybody is obliged to conform and is unable to get away without being castigated, as is possible in an environment of extreme social, economic and political inequalities, and of common, uninhibited violation of social mores. The other factor was the difficulties faced by people in a war-ravaged economy. Everyone knew clearly what national reconstruction required — economy in the use of resources. This realisation provided a binding authority to the cultural values of simple living and abstinence from conspicuous consumption,[75] thus leading to their unchallenged observance by all without exception. Individual families tended to be extremely frugal.

This helped moderate consumption and generate a high rate of saving in these countries. Gross domestic saving as a percent of gross domestic product was 33.4, 30.7, 39.9, 37.6, and 37.0 percent in Japan, Hong Kong, Singapore, South Korea, and Taiwan respectively in 1987 as compared with the average of 19.8 percent for Latin America and the Caribbean, 13.0 percent for Sub-Saharan Africa, 17.0 percent for the Middle East and North Africa, and 19.3 percent for South Asia.[76] The high rate of saving provided the domestic resources needed for capital formation and expansion of output and exports.

The contribution that this high rate of saving has made to the economic success of these countries should not be underestimated. It kept the interest rates in those countries relatively lower than elsewhere and thus encouraged investment. It enabled the government as well as the private sector finance their investments without resort, as in other developing countries, to unduly large monetary and credit expansion and external borrowing. This kept inflation under control and enhanced their competitiveness in the export market. It also enabled them to enlarge their productive capacity and laid the foundation for the success of their outward-looking policy without loading their economies with a high debt-servicing burden as has happened in other developing countries.

Import Control and Export Promotion

While the social values have helped promote savings in these countries, they have also helped substantially in restraining inessential imports. In other developing countries this legitimate national need has been fulfilled by high import tariffs and stiff exchange controls, which lead to smuggling, under-invoicing and corruption. In the non-legal consensus societies of these countries, the need was satisfied by social norms which it is not possible to violate without being socially castigated. Therefore, while it might seem that these economies were outward-oriented they were so primarily in terms of exports and not imports, even though the absence of strict import controls may make them appear to be so.[77] Moreover, as Lester Thurow has observed with respect to Japan: "How does a foreign firm break in as a new supplier of industrial components, for example, when Japanese firms place a premium on maintaining long-term intimate supply relationships with nearby suppliers in the just-in-time inventory system?" [78]

Moreover, the role of outward-orientation in these countries is being unduly overemphasised. Export-led growth is new to Japan. In the 1950s and 1960s Japan had a chronic trade deficit. Companies became successful by winning at home and then, by exploiting economies of sale, to venture overseas: domestic demand fuelled the export drive, not the other way round.

Korea, Taiwan and a number of countries which have succeeded in promoting their exports have "all initially followed the import-substitution path".[79]

All these countries resorted to a substantial degree of protection initially, and only later on was there a shift from import-substitution to export promotion, but without any significant change in the development philosophy. They were almost forced to do so because their limited foreign exchange earnings had to be diverted to the purchase of foreign technology and machinery which they could not initially produce themselves. The whole economy was organized to minimise imports of non-essential goods. While protection is not sufficient for successful industrialisation, the argument that it is not necessary seems largely an *a priori* assumption. Most historical examples from Germany and the U.S. to Japan have involved protection. Even now, all these countries resort to a substantial degree of protection with respect to both industry and agriculture. Asking developing countries to do what even the developed countries have themselves not done, and are not doing, is unrealistic advice.

Low Defence Spending

A distinguishing feature of Japanese public finance has been the low level of spending on defence. Military spending has been held down to less than one percent of GNP compared with an average of around four percent in industrial countries and about three percent in developing countries.[80] This has realised resources for building an efficient infrastructure in spite of the relatively low level of total government spending. It has also helped keep taxes at a lower level compared with other countries. In Japan, taxes constituted 21 percent of GDP in 1975 and 31.3 percent in 1988 compared with 33 percent and 40.8 percent respectively in the EEC.[81] While South Korea and Taiwan have maintained a higher profile in defence spending as compared with Japan, their fiscal burden has been substantially reduced by foreign aid, primarily from the United States.

A PEEP INTO THE FUTURE

One may thus see clearly the decisive role that a number of factors have played in the rapid growth of these countries, particularly in reducing the conflict between the objectives of growth and equity. It would, therefore, be improper to attribute the credit for all these factors to liberalisation alone, even though liberalisation has also played an important role. A crucial question that one may wish to raise here is whether it would be possible for these countries to sustain the equity that they were able to realise due to exceptional circumstances? Some of the factors that have been eroding equity in these countries lead one to a negative answer.

South Korea, unlike Taiwan, opted for large family-run conglomerates (chaebol) in the industrial sector. The chaebol have continually grown bigger with the help of Government and financing from banks. By 1984, the 10 largest chaebol accounted for 64 percent of GNP and 70 percent of exports.[82] Even though preference for labour-intensive techniques generated a substantial expansion in employment opportunities, these became available mainly in urban centres and not in rural areas. Consequently, unlike Taiwan, there was a large shift of population from rural areas to urban centres.[83] Almost half of the country's population is now crammed in four major urban centres (Seoul, Pusan, Taegu and Inchon). This has led to a pressure on housing and other facilities in these urban centres, making the life of rural migrants miserable. The chaebol, helped in their expansion by the urban bias and the banking system, have tended to widen income disparities in South Korea. In 1965, the share of income of the bottom 93 percent was 19.3 percent, but by 1987 it had declined to 16.9 percent — that of the top 20 percent had risen to 45.3 percent from 41.8 percent.[84]

Thus even though income distribution is more equitable in South Korea than in comparable developing countries, the choice of chaebol as the preferred form of business organisation has sown the seeds of income disparity, conspicuous consumption and industrial strife. From 1981 to 1985, there were only 100 strikes a year. In 1986, there were 276. But in 1987 the number of strikes shot up to 3008.[85] This indicates that the growing inequalities and hardships faced by migrant labour in urban areas is eroding the harmonious industrial relationship fostered by the socio-economic equality created by land reforms and cultural values. "For three decades Korea sought economic development regardless of the social consequences. Attitudes are now changing".[86] Parvez Hasan has thus rightly remarked that "the past experience of lagging rural income and excessive migration to urban areas has underscored the need for a comprehensive strategy to deal with the economic imbalance of rural and urban areas".[87]

In Japan also, the prognosis for the future is a gradual increase in inequalities. The post-War dissolution of Zaibatsu (family-controlled groups of monopolistic companies like Mitsui, Mitsubishi, Sumitomo and Yasuda) along with land reforms spread economic power more evenly over the population, making it difficult for a small group of people to dominate the national economy and politics.

This led to a proliferation of small- and medium-scale enterprises and created intense competition in all industries. Efficiency increased, making it possible for Japan to be competitive internationally. However, the law which led to their abolition (The Elimination of Excessive Concentration of Economic Power Law) became a dead letter from the late 1940s onwards and was finally repealed in the mid-1950s. This rendered ineffective the dissolution of Zaibatsu, as is evident from the rise of the Mitsubishi, Mitsui and Sumitomo companies virtually to their previous positions.[88] Even though these companies are now structured quite differently from their Zaibatsu days, they still exercise considerable economic and political clout. The Zaibatsu banks, which have been gradually becoming more powerful, have become the hand-maidens of these companies, and it is most likely that their hold on the economy will increase, gradually but continually.[89]

While it is true that small businesses proliferate in Japan, they now account for a much smaller share of sales.[90] Besides, most of these firms are company-affiliated stores not having the freedom to set their own prices. Thus, the system, aided by the banking setup, is gradually leading to concentration of wealth which, even though it may not be of the same nature and intensity as that of the Zaibatsu days, is moving closer to it.[91] No wonder Japan already has six of the world's ten richest men even though only four decades have passed since the near elimination of inequalities after the War.[92] Such excessively rich people are able to exercise, as in other countries, an increasing influence on the economy and the polity.[93] The process of ongoing liberalisation may intensify concentration, particularly if the Agricultural Land Act, which has prevented the revival of landlord system, and the Large-Scale Retail Store Law, which has impeded the entry of large stores into the retail sector, are repealed or diluted significantly.

A substantial part of the savings in these countries are now going into stock market and land speculation and boosting share and land values, thus providing momentum to the trend towards concentration. The Nikkei index rose from an average of 102 in 1950 to 1,117 in 1960, 2,193 in 1970, 6,870 in 1980, and 26,646 just before the October 1987 crash. Prices, however, recovered faster in Japan than in any other major stock market and the index rose to the high of 38,916 in December 1989.[94]

The Japanese stock market has thus seen share prices double on average every four years. The average price/earnings ratio for Japanese equities has accordingly risen from 10.7 in 1970 to 19.1 in 1980 and the high of 61.4 in April 1988. Thereafter it declined to 50.4 in July 1989 due primarily to a rise in interest rates. Comparative price/earnings ratios for other major countries in July 1989 were: United States, 13.3; United Kingdom, 11.7; West Germany, 15.7; and France, 12.5.[95] The dizzying height of the Japanese price-earnings ratio carries the seeds of a serious crisis, which could unfold at any time and have an extremely destabilising effect not only on the Japanese economy but also on the world financial markets.

Land values have also risen steeply. The average price of land for commercial, residential and industrial use in six major cities has doubled on an average every four years taking the index of average land prices from 100 in March 1955 to 12,848 in 1989.[96] Commercial, residential and industrial properties have hence become so expensive in Japan that they are now beyond the reach of most middle-class families.

This shatters their dream of one day owning their own business and a home. The high cost of office and residential property also adds high premium to all goods and services purchased by the Japanese, thus reducing their real income. Japan has now become one of the most expensive countries in the world. The internal purchasing power of the Yen has thus been outstripped by its exchange rate.

Speculation in both shares and property, nevertheless, continues to be fanned by credit extended for this purpose by banks to those who have the collateral. Since the value of the collateral (shares and property) was escalating, credit was also expanding simultaneously. The speculative boom was thus accentuating wealth inequalities and deeply eroding the socio-economic equity that had been realised after the War. This time the shares- and property-owing *nouveaux riches* have different attitudes. They are indulging in conspicuous consumption, thus increasing social inequalities and loosening the social glue that strengthened social solidarity.[97] The same speculative boom with its adverse effect on socio-economic equality is also taking place in both South Korea and Taiwan.[98]

Thus, even though these countries started after the War with relative equality, which made it possible for them to realise growth with justice, they have found it difficult to sustain this equality within the framework of the capitalist economic and financial systems that prevail in these countries.

This shows that even if inequalities are minimised initially by unusual circumstances, they would re-emerge and lead to concentration of wealth unless the total economy is restructured and the financial system is reorganised in a way that would help to sustain as well as promote equity. Important elements of such a restructuring, particularly of the financial system, which has a strong tendency to promote concentration of wealth, will be addressed in chapter 4 on the Islamic strategy of development.

THE MISSING LINK

Thus, while the Far Eastern countries have, to a large extent, been able to attain higher growth with equity, it would be a mistake to overemphasise the role of liberalisation in this achievement. Even neo-classical economists accept that "the emphasis on the market did not mean that the government must accept the practice and results of *laissez-faire,* but rather that the government should improve and strengthen the market price system".[99] The answer to the question whether neo-classical liberalisation, along with the 'improvement' and 'strengthening' of the market system by the government, can sustain equity is negative, as discussed above.

The primary reason for greater equity in Far Eastern countries is not liberalisation but rather exceptional circumstances which prevailed in these countries after the War, government polices and cultural values. Such a combination of equity-creating circumstances cannot be duplicated in other developing countries under normal peace-time conditions. Without the socio-economic equality that these factors created, neo-classical liberalisation will only worsen the equity picture unless it is accompanied by an effective strategy for advancing the cause of equity.

Even though such cultural values are also present in other countries, their effectiveness has been blunted by the prevailing high level of socio-economic inequality, continued moral degeneration, and the onslaught of

Western consumer culture. Hence the challenge that faces us is how to realise and sustain equity in countries where it has not been created by force of circumstances.

Development economics, in spite of reintroducing equity as a goal, has been unable, uptil now, to propose an effective strategy for realising it in countries which do not have the same enabling environment that was created by exceptional circumstances in the Far East. As Morawetz has pertinently indicated after a study of twenty-five years of development: "There exists a vast and easily accessible literature on the subject of how to grow: on what policies have been tried, where and with what results. But on the question of how to redistribute, the contributions though many are more disparate".[100] Even though this statement was made more than a decade ago, it is still true. Reliance continues to be primarily on growth for improving distribution. But as Fields has rightly concluded:

> Although rapid economic growth generally reduces poverty, growth
> is neither necessary nor sufficient for poverty alleviation. . . .
> Whether inequality increases or decreases with economic growth
> depends on the type of growth rather than on the level of GNP or
> the rate of GNP growth *per se*.[101]

The continued poverty of development economics in suggesting an effective programme for reducing inequalities gives the impression that even the concern for equity that is now being expressed may be temporary and "just one more fashion in a fashion-prone discipline".[102] This feeling is further reinforced by the widening circle of neo-classical economists who would prefer equity to remain an indirect goal of policy rather than become a direct, express and fundamental goal. For them, the 'poverty' of development economics lies not in its indirect and inadequate discussion of equity, but rather in its getting involved in such a discussion.[103]

An effective strategy for realising equity requires socially-agreed values, a motivating system and economic restructuring. These are not attainable within the value-free framework of neo-classical economics. If appropriate policies can be suggested, why should or why would others accept them? As Meier has rightly indicated, the most underdeveloped part of development economics is the question of "how to gain the acceptance of more appropriate policies?"[104] Why, one may ask, is it relatively easy to suggest policies but extremely difficult to gain their acceptance and implementation? The reason is, as Meier has again indicated, that there is "a rare public policy from which everyone gains. Some in the country will gain and some will lose from the policy action."[105] It is hence necessary to have a mechanism by which to motivate even those who will be worse off to accept the policies suggested.

Neo-classical economics fails here. It can be effective only as long as the question is that of serving everyone's self-interest, which is necessary to induce greater initiative and efficiency. But equitable distribution cannot be attained by everyone serving just his self-interest; such behaviour in fact tends to worsen income distribution. Equitable distribution requires a motivation to serve social interest even if this involves sacrifice of self-interest. Social interest will be served under the neo-classical model only as long as it coincides with self-interest. The secularist value-free approach of liberalism does not have any mechanism to motivate people to sacrifice self-interest for social interest when the two do not coincide. According to a World Bank Report, if incomes were distributed differently at the global level, the present output of grain alone could supply every man, woman and child with more than 3,000 calories and 65 grams of protein per day — far more than the highest estimates of requirements.[106] Compared with this, the daily calorie supply per capita was lower in 1985 than in 1965 in most developing countries.[107]

Needs remain unsatisfied, not necessarily because of lack of resources to produce a sufficient quantity of need-satisfying goods, but because of inequitable distribution of wealth. The neo-classical model is not capable of bringing about an equitable distribution; had it been, it would have succeeded in the rich industrial countries with their far greater resources and growth, and the Development Committee would not have been led to admit that "it has proved extremely difficult to address poverty problems successfully".[108]

It was the failure of the neo-classical model to promote equity which gave birth to socialism. But socialism also failed to promote equity in most countries; it had the added disadvantage that in almost all countries it also failed to promote efficiency. Since equity is the most urgent socio-political imperative of developing countries, the present revival of neo-classical economics cannot be expected to promote what it has failed to do in the past.

Inequities may hence be expected to persist in developing countries if they revert to the neo-classical model. This carries the potential of further exacerbating discontent, which has already heightened in recent years. The political upheaval that this may initiate may tend to tilt the balance once again in favour of anti-liberalism, this time with a vengeance. But will such a revival of anti-liberalism succeed in promoting equity in developing countries when it has failed to do so in the past in both the developing and most socialist countries? Probably not. Hence, instead of being swung like a football by the two systems from one extreme to the other, the developing countries need to develop their own strategy in the light of their own socio-economic imperatives.

FOUR

THE ISLAMIC STRATEGY

The Islamic world-view, as discussed in chapter 1, makes it a moral imperative of every Muslim society to try its utmost to foster brotherhood and socio-economic justice, such that their realisation, and not their absence, become the dominant characteristic of that society. In the economic field, this necessitates development with justice and stability to attain general need-fulfilment, full employment, and equitable distribution of income and wealth, without unduly large or prolonged imbalances.

Given the resource constraint and the prevailing imbalances, the pursuit of such development is not possible without a substantial decline in claims on resources along with their reallocation from less efficient and less equitable uses to more efficient and more equitable uses. As discussed in chapters 2 and 3, such a reallocation cannot be realised within the value-neutral and this-worldly framework of any secularist system in spite of excessive government intervention in the economy. The Islamic strategy has, however, a greater potential for success because of its four very effective and interrelated elements.

IMPORTANT ELEMENTS OF THE STRATEGY

1. EQUITABLE FILTERING OF EXCESS CLAIMS

The first problem that every society faces in actualising its egalitarian goals is how to filter out the unlimited claims on scarce resources in such a way that only those claims are left which would pass the tests of both efficiency and equity. It has already been shown that, while the price mechanism does perform the filtering function, it does not do so in an equitable manner. Islam, therefore, complements it by adding another filter which helps ensure equity.

The moral filter attacks the problem of unlimited wants at the very source — the inner consciousness of the individuals — by changing their preference scales in accordance with social priorities and making their claims on resources a function of human well-being. It eliminates, or at least minimises, the claims that are inessential and inequitable from the point of view of realising social goals. It does not, for example, permit the use of resources for morally prohibited activities — activities that would only kill or harm human beings, animals or plants, either now or in the future and thereby reduce their well-being. It requires a modest life-style and does not allow extravagance or the use of resources for ostentation or vain consumption — uses that do not make a real difference in human well-being. It also does not permit the destruction, or wasteful use, of resources (e.g., burning food to raise prices). It also reorganises financial intermediation so as to enable it to play a role that is complementary to that of the price filter in helping keep claims on resources within the limits of humanity.

The moral filter thus moderates and humanises the influence that wealth and power and financial intermediation are able to exercise in the allocation and distribution of resources. The introduction of the moral filter implies the evaluation of claims on scarce resources in the light of socially-agreed moral values even before the claims are expressed in the market place. After all claims on resources have been passed through the moral filter, and unnecessary and inequitable claims thus eliminated or minimised, the price filter of the market system takes over. The price filter can then perform more effectively the task of bringing about the allocation of resources that is both efficient and equitable.

2. MOTIVATION

The second problem that every society faces is how to motivate individuals to serve the social interest in conformity with the moral filter even when doing so hurts their self-interest. This is because all individuals wish to serve their self-interest and, unless they are able to do so, their behaviour will not be conducive to the realisation of optimum efficiency in the use of resources. Any effort to prevent the individuals from serving their self-interest, as socialism tried to do, is bound to fail. What Adam Smith did to overcome the conflict between the two interests was to try to show that the serving of self-interest by every individual also served the social interest.

Since this is not necessarily true, as we have already shown, therefore, in order to realise the harmonization of individual and social interests, the individuals should be made to recognise the opposite of what Adam Smith said — that the serving of social interest also serves their self-interest. This is the approach of Islam. Islam does not prevent the individual from serving his self-interest, but by giving self-interest a spiritual, long-term perspective — extending its span beyond this life. Even if it is accepted that the individual's self-interest in this world may be served by being selfish and unscrupulous, his interest in the Hereafter cannot be served except by behaving in a way that does not hurt the interests of others who, being the vicegerents of God like him, are his equals and brothers, and whose needs must be satisfied through a fair share in God-given resources.

Islam, on the one hand, recognises the contribution that self-interest and the desire for profit can make towards individual initiative, drive, efficiency and entrepreneurship. On the other hand, the evils of greed, unscrupulousness and disregard for the rights and needs of others, which the secularist and short-term this-worldly perspective of both capitalism and socialism tend to promote, are overcome by introducing an internal self-regulating mechanism with its unrelenting emphasis on belief in God, moral values, accountability before Him, human brotherhood, and socio-economic justice.

The idea of accountability before the Supreme Being can serve as a strong motivating force in inducing individuals to abide by moral values and in preventing them from pursuing self-interest beyond the limits of social health and well-being. Competition and market forces, which according to Adam Smith, performed this function, are undoubtedly essential for playing a complementary role, but are not effective enough to ensure the interest and well-being of *all*. This is because: firstly, competition can also be unhealthy, and secondly, this-worldly self-interest, unhindered by moral compunctions, may tend to find different ways of restraining competition and thwarting the operation of market forces, particularly when wealth and power are also unequally distributed.

3. SOCIO-ECONOMIC RESTRUCTURING

Values may, nevertheless, be violated and the idea of accountability before God may, in many cases, be too feeble to have much impact on human behaviour. Even in a morally-charged society, individuals may tend to be oblivious to the problems of scarcity and to social priorities in resource allocation, if the socio-economic environment is not conducive. They may simply be unaware of the urgent and unsatisfied needs of others, and, if they are well-to-do, may unconsciously follow unhealthy social trends and divert scarce resources away from the need fulfilment of others, in order to satisfy their relatively less urgent wants.

It is necessary, therefore, to reinforce moral values by socio-economic restructuring in such manner that individuals find it possible to serve their self-interest, only within the constraints of social well-being and economic stability. The restructuring must address itself to:

a)   transforming the human factor in development to enable it to play an active and constructive role in the efficient and equitable allocation of resources;

b)   reducing the existing concentration in the ownership of means of production as much as possible to complement the role of moral transformation in minimising the influence of wealth and power in the allocation and distribution of resources;

c)   eliminating or minimising all 'wasteful' and 'unnecessary' consumption at the private as well as the public level to raise savings and to make a larger volume of resources available for investment and need fulfilment;

d)   reforming the financial system in a way that would enable it to play a complementary and enabling role in the above restructuring.

4. ROLE OF THE STATE

Such a restructuring may not take place effectively unless all forces involved in it act in a concerted manner. The government must also, therefore, play a positive, goal-oriented role in the economy. This is not the kind of role that would lead to the establishment of a totalitarian order as happened in the USSR, China and other communist block countries. It is rather a complementary role which is to be played by the government through the internalisation of Islamic values in society, the creation of a healthy socio-economic environment, and the development of proper enabling institutions, and not through excessive controls, unnecessary violation of individual freedom, and abolition of property rights.

FIVE POLICY MEASURES

This four-dimensional approach of Islam (complementing the price mechanism by the moral filter, motivating the individual to take the social interest into account, socio-economic restructuring, and positive role of the government) should prove to be more effective in ensuring the well-being of all than the single-dimensional capitalist or socialist approach of relying solely either on self-interest and market forces or solely on collectivisation and central planning. In contrast with this, the governments in poorer Muslim countries have, in general, been inwardly (though not outwardly) secular, in step with the conventional wisdom borrowed by them from the Western secular culture which occupies a dominant place in the present-day world. They have thus been unable to formulate a strategy for development with justice.

Their policies have, therefore, lacked a firm direction and have oscillated on the waves of socialism and free enterprise, and controls and decontrols that have been in vogue in development literature over the last four decades. This lack of firm direction, combined with fluctuations and inconsistencies in policies, has generated uncertainties and caused immense harm to the developmental process. Whatever development has been achieved has been at a high cost in terms of macroeconomic imbalances, increased inequalities of incomes and wealth, and social tensions.

What the Muslim countries need, therefore, is to move away from the secular and inconsistent approach of Development Economics and to reformulate their policies within the framework of the integrated approach of Islam. However, while reformulating policies within this framework, it is neither possible nor necessary to find a precedent for all of them in the early Islamic history. Although the *Sharī'ah* has prescribed the essential elements of a basic strategy, it has allowed flexibility over space and time by not spelling out detailed policy measures. These have to be developed. It may be possible to emulate the experience of other countries with respect to specific policies.

But, while doing so, it is necessary to ensure that the policy measures being considered for adoption fulfil two criteria — that they make a positive contribution towards the realisation of the *maqāṣid* without coming into conflict with the *Sharī'ah*, and that they do not lead to an excessive increase in the claims on resources. The second criterion should not be fulfilled within the framework of Pareto optimality. A strategy that concerns itself with increasing resources for a specific purpose without effectively reducing its availability for other purposes, can only lead to frustrations and imbalances.

Value neutrality must hence be set aside. Policies must be passed through the filter of Islamic values. The testing of all policy measures against these criteria will strengthen the hand of governments in getting the policies publicly accepted, particularly policies which do not satisfy the criterion of Pareto optimality.

Five policy measures are suggested below for development combined with justice and stability. These are: (1) invigorating the human factor; (2) reducing concentration of wealth; (3) economic restructuring; (4) financial restructuring; and (5) strategic policy planning. Some of these policy measures may be familiar to those well-versed in development literature. What is important, however, is the injection of a moral dimension into all material parameters of development. Without such an integration of the moral and the material, it may not be possible to realise either efficiency or equity as defined earlier.

1. INVIGORATING THE HUMAN FACTOR

Human beings constitute the living and indispensable element of any development programme. They constitute the end as well as the means of development, and unless they are reformed suitably to enable them to make a positive contribution to development and to keep their self-interest within the constraints of social well-being, nothing else can succeed in actualising the basic objectives of Islam. Hence, the most challenging task before Muslim countries is to motivate the human factor to do all that is necessary in the interest of development with justice. Individuals must be willing to render their best by working hard and efficiently with integrity, conscientiousness and discipline, and to make the sacrifices necessary to overcome obstacles in the path of development. They must also be willing to change their consumption, saving and investment behaviour in conformity with what is required to raise the rate of growth with greater equity and lower imbalances.

Motivation alone is, however, not sufficient to get the best out of human beings. They must also have the ability to use better technology and management methods. This requires proper training and access to finance. Unless an adequate arrangement is made for both, motivation alone may not be able to take the economic system far in realising the optimum potential of the human factor.

MOTIVATION

To motivate individuals to render their best and to utilise the scarce resources with maximum efficiency, it is necessary that their self-interest be served by doing so. Socialism was naive and unrealistic when it expected individuals to work efficiently even though it deprived them of the opportunity to serve their self-interest. It therefore failed. Capitalism is also unrealistic in its assumption that self-interest and social interest are always in harmony. Its secularism and this-worldly perspective do not provide any mechanism for motivating individuals to serve the social interest when this is in conflict with their self-interest.

Experience has established beyond every shadow of doubt that it is not possible to motivate individuals to be both efficient and equitable unless a moral dimension is injected into their pursuit of self-interest so that social interest is not jeopardised even when it is in conflict with self-interest.

However, there is a two-way link between moral strength and socio-economic justice; it is not possible to realise one without simultaneous progress in the realisation of the other. In Muslim countries where the moral strength of the society is being sapped by socio-economic injustice, it would be unrealistic to depend primarily on sermons to raise moral consciousness; it is necessary to remove the inequities and to establish justice by a thorough restructuring of the economy and the society. Hence, the question of realising justice needs to be addressed even before the imperative of moral transformation is discussed.

Socio-Economic Justice

Material rewards have become so inequitable that most people are unable to get a due reward for their hard work, creativity, and contribution to output. They have consequently become apathetic and their initiative, drive and efficiency have all suffered considerably. There are two factors responsible for this: firstly, the lack of realism in official policies, and secondly, concentration of wealth and power in a few hands in both rural and urban areas. The lack of realism in official policies has led to distortion of key prices which unconsciously result in lowering the incomes of tenant farmers, small and micro enterprises (SMEs), and workers, reducing their demand for needs and creating a misallocation of resources against need-fulfilment. The concentration of wealth and power, also due partly to official policies and partly to the exploitative economic system that has prevailed for centuries, has restricted competition and created a climate conducive to the misery of the rural and urban poor. This has reduced their willingness and ability to do their best.

Rural Uplift

The unrealism of official policies is fully reflected in the lack of emphasis on rural development. While a preponderant proportion of the population of Muslim countries lives in rural areas, official policies have placed undue emphasis on urban development and on the establishment of large-scale enterprises in urban areas, and neglected the development of human, physical and financial infrastructure in rural areas. This has not only reduced the rewards for the effort of tenant-farmers and rural workers but also lowered their ability to invest in better seeds, fertilisers and equipment and in SMEs to supplement their incomes from agriculture. It has also led to an influx of labour to urban areas, thereby depressing wages and living conditions there.

In contrast with this, the heavy protection, concessionary financing and subsidised inputs given to large-scale urban businessess and industries has raised the comparative advantage of such urban enterprises, reduced the competitiveness of rural and urban SMEs, and enhanced the concentration of wealth and power. While high tax evasion prevents the governments from reaping the benefit of urban development, the urban congestion lowers the wages and salaries of urban employees, prevents them from being appropriately rewarded for their contribution to urban prosperity, and lowers their ability to save and invest.

It is, therefore, necessary to introduce realism in official policies by removing the bias against the development of agriculture and SMEs. This is, however, not enough. It is also necessary to introduce a number of socio-economic reforms that would help raise the real incomes of all workers, savers, investors and exporters, and particularly so if they are poor.

Labour Reforms

Islamic values require employers to consider employees as members of their own family. This demands that employees be treated with respect and compassion and that their well-being be ensured. Real wages in a Muslim society should ideally be at least at a level that would enable employees to fulfil all their, and their families' essential needs properly.[1] They must also be provided with training, job security and, preferably, also a share in profits within the framework of a long-term, harmonious relationship.

In sharp contrast with this, real wages in most Muslim countries are so low that, in spite of nearly 10—14 hours of hard work, a labourer is unable to meet his own and his family's basic needs. In addition, employees do not enjoy any job security. The reasons for this are not merely low productivity, excess supply of labour, and lack of adequate opportunities for employment, as the neo-classical economists would have us believe. A substantial role is played by exploitation, which is made possible by a configuration of unjust forces, including inappropriate official policies, concentration of wealth and power, and lack of training and financing facilities for workers. Unless the forces of exploitation are substantially weakened, it may not be possible to do justice to workers and to induce them to work conscientiously and efficiently.

The prescription of minimum wages may not, nevertheless, be the immediate solution. It would be difficult to enforce and, if enforced, it could have two adverse effects. Firstly, it could lead to a difference in wages as reported to the authorities and those actually paid. This would imply a reduction in the tax liability of the employer without any real benefit to the labourer. Secondly, it could exacerbate the prevailing high level of unemployment.

It would hence be better to resort to an entirely different package of policies — policies that would blunt the edge of exploitation firstly, by raising the productivity of workers, and secondly, by expanding the opportunities available for self-employment in both rural and urban areas. Such policies should include: a) provision of better vocational training to raise productivity; b) extension of financing facilities to promote SMEs; and c) restructuring of the entire economy in favour of need fulfilment and a more equitable distribution of incomes and wealth. These policies should be further reinforced by making profit-sharing schemes as widespread as possible for enabling the employees to share in the profits of their firms.

Every firm should be required to implement a profit-sharing scheme for employees. A certain agreed proportion of the firm's net profit should be required to be partly allocated for distribution among the employees as profit-sharing bonus and partly utilised to provide training facilities, to improve their working conditions, and grant medical benefits, educational allowances for children, housing facilities, and food subsidies.

Linking the increase in income and benefits of employees beyond a certain minimum needed for comfortable living to their firm's profitability, should have a number of benefits. These would include: a) reduction in the existing apathy through a boost in the employees' morale, thus leading to greater conscientiousness, less wastage and higher productivity; b) improvement in labour-management relations through worker participation in management, thus helping revive an important characteristic of an ideal Muslim society; c) keeping the employees' earnings flexible and responsive to the health of the national economy and the performance of their firms — the employees sharing amply in their firm's prosperity when profits are good but not being laid off when profits are low or the firm is suffering losses; d) reduction in tax evasion (provided that the tax system is reformed), because the employees, in their own self-interest, would keep an eye on the firm's actual profits with respect to which they are currently indifferent; and e) increase in the competitiveness of the economy and the firms, thus improving the general climate for investment and the macro-economic performance of the economy. While implementing the profit-sharing scheme, it is necessary to ensure that this policy does not lead to exploitation. This could happen if the minimum wage, which is not subject to risk, is not adequate to meet the basic needs of the employee.

The employees' share of profit, in addition to being distributed in the form of cash bonuses, subsidies and services, could also be distributed in the form of shares to implement an Employee Stock Ownership Plan (ESOP). The introduction of ESOP can enable workers to become equity owners and can go a long way towards reducing concentration of wealth and power. It will enable workers to participate actively in the firm's management and motivate them to be more conscientious and efficient. It will also help reduce industrial strife. It will raise savings, discourage the unproductive alternative of gold-hoarding and also help raise their social status in the company and society. ESOP has been adopted in even some capitalist countries like France, the U.K. and the U.S.A., and there is no reason why it should not receive enthusiastic support in Muslim countries.

Fair Return to Small Depositors and Shareholders

The low rates of return on deposits and shares in many Muslim countries, the result of administrative fiats and corporate corruption, hurt mainly the small savers and investors. Big businesses use various devices to get their due return. They are, besides, alleged to keep most of their savings abroad to evade taxes, to protect themselves from the depreciation of the national currency, and to get a higher international market-related return. They do, however, borrow from local banks and government financial institutions at lower prime or concessionary rates for domestic investment. This accentuates inequalities.

This is not a plea in favour of higher interest rates, which hurt investment, but rather a strong case in favour of equity financing and reform of banks and non-bank corporations in conformity with the objectives of the Shari'ah. This will not only enable savers and investors to get a just reward but will also help bring about greater allocative 'efficiency', economic stability and growth.[2]

Justice to Producers, Exporters, and Consumers

Similarly, unrealistic exchange rates and unnecessary price controls hurt producers and exporters, while high protective tariffs hurt consumers. The plea that these measures serve the interest of the common man and promote the country's development is usually a facade. They do not. They, rather, serve the vested interest of the rich and the powerful who have been continuously growing richer at the expense of the masses who have become more and more impoverished. They also prevent the authorities from adopting healthy policies that would curb inflation, expand the supply of need-satisfying goods and services, and expand employment and incomes.

All measures that enrich a minority of the population at the expense of the majority cannot be defended in the light of the Shari'ah. It is necessary, however, to take adequate measures to safeguard the interest of the poor before the exchange rates are realigned and price controls are removed. Such measures may take different forms, including income supplements or relief payments out of zakāh and other funds earmarked for this purpose, accompanied by incentives and facilities to expand the supply of need-fulfilling goods and services and income-earning opportunities.

Moral Transformation

Although a *quid pro quo* relationship between work and reward is indispensable for eliciting hard and efficient work, it is not necessarily sufficient for inducing integrity and conscientiousness. It is also not adequate to motivate people to change their consumption, saving and investment behaviour in conformity with what is required for actualising socio-economic goals. Secularism, which, for quite some time, has tacitly been the dominant philosophy in most of the Muslim countries, regardless of their leaning towards socialism or capitalism, fails to provide the filter mechanism necessary to serve social goals as well as the charisma that would inspire people and motivate them to make the sacrifices required.

Islam, however, has a great potential for creating the desired qualities in people and for making them identify social interest with their personal interest. It not only demands these characteristics in its followers, it also possesses the necessary charisma to inspire and change them.[3]

However, since the Muslim masses have, to a considerable extent, lost touch with the inner core of their faith owing to the decline which seized the Muslim societies in general domination, the implementation of a reform programme based on Islamic values is indispensable. It would help accelerate development substantially in Muslim countries by improving the quality and preferences of the human factor.

Fears may be expressed here about the cost and the time span involved in moral transformation. Such fears seem to be exaggerated. The implementing machinery already exists in the form of mosques (which exist even in the remotest villages of Muslim countries), educational institutions, news media and social reform organisations.

If all these are properly mobilised and effectively utilised for improving the quality of the human resources, the cost may not be very high. The governments need to get the *imām*s (prayer leaders) of the mosques, school teachers and social workers involved in the whole process of social change through their proper training and the preparation of necessary literature. The preparation of this literature may also not require a stupendous effort because, in addition to what is contained in the Qur'ān and the *Sunnah*, a great deal has been written, over the centuries, on the character of a true Muslim and his responsibility before God and fellow human beings. Hence an important task that the governments need to perform is to have this material put across in a simple, effective manner through the network of existing institutions, to mobilise the energies of the people for socio-economic reform and development.

Fears about the time span are, however, realistic. But, if moral reform is necessary for socio-economic development, then an effort has to be made in that direction. The lack of willingness to initiate the process of social change through moral reform will not reduce the time span. Changing the social mood may help reduce the time span substantially.

Reform movements have been trying to accomplish this in Muslim countries but have not been able to make much headway because of the virtual apathy of, in fact antagonism from, governments. If the governments shed their secular tendency and throw their full weight behind the reform movements, the social mood may change faster and provide the needed momentum to social change; ultimately leading to the desired quality of people. If this is not done, the erosion in morals will continue and contribute to a further degeneration in the quality of people accompanied by its adverse impact on development and socio-political stability.

The effective use of educational institutions and news media may help the governments accelerate the pace of social change and eliminate or reduce more rapidly the hold of a number of un-Islamic social values (like conspicuous consumption and ostentatious ceremonies) that put a heavy strain on resources and hurt the realisation of the *maqāṣid*. Such values vitiate the social environment and lead to a consumption pattern that hurts development and need fulfilment. Unless the governments throw their full weight behind social reform, and apply Islamic values uniformly to all — rich or poor, high or low — it may not be possible to bring about the needed social change.

ABILITY

While socio-economic justice, moral consciousness, and proper social environment are all necessary to motivate people, they are not enough to realise 'efficiency' and 'equity'. Two persons may be equally motivated, yet they may be unable to contribute equally to the realisation of the *maqāṣid*. The difference lies in ability which is not only inborn but also acquired, partly through education and training and partly through access to finance.

Expansion of educational and training facilities and access of the poor to finance are hence indispensable.

Education and Training

The invaluable contribution that appropriate education and training can make towards improvement in the quality of human beings, greater socio-economic justice, and faster growth is now universally recognised. Education opens the door to social equality and economic opportunity, and has been rightly considered to be the great equaliser of human conditions.

Many Muslim governments have nevertheless been conspicuously guilty of neglecting this important sector in their resource allocation. Even literacy, which is the first step on the path of education, has not become universal in most Muslim countries. Of particular significance is the neglect of female education, on which depends the character, health and ability of both the present and the future generations. Such neglect cannot continue for long without ruining the fabric of the contemporary Muslim society.

The primary stress of education has to be on creating a 'good' and 'productive' human being. This is what will help mobilise the large pools of zeal and talent that remain untapped in Muslim countries. Every Muslim student should be taught the qualities of a true Muslim and should be strongly motivated to create those qualities in himself. But this is not sufficient. It is also necessary to teach him the skills in demand and the most efficient techniques of production, management and marketing.

The secular educational system in vogue in most Muslim countries has not only failed to make the students better human beings, enriched by the characteristics of a true Muslim and conscious of their responsibilities towards society, but has also failed to make them more productive by teaching them the skills in demand. While qualified young men are unable to get admission in vocational training institutes and engineering and medical colleges due to shortage of facilities, the universities, following loyally the conventional syllabi bequeathed to them by the colonial masters, have been producing generations of secularised liberal arts majors for clerical and civil service jobs, which have now become more than fully saturated. There is thus a steep rise in the number of 'educated unemployed' in urban areas in spite of a scarcity of trained manpower in several sectors of the economy. While the rich are easily able to get technical education for their children at home and abroad, the poor, who need it more acutely to raise their income and social status, are unable to do so. This tends to widen the gulf between the rich and the poor, and to condemn the poor to a position of permanent misery. This is a clear indictment of the educational systems for not responding positively to the changing economic and political realities of Muslim countries.

There is, therefore, a dire need for a substantial change in educational curricula with a view to inculcate Islamic values and impart the needed technical skills. It is also necessary to establish a widespread network of institutions so that even a poor man's child in a rural area or urban slum shall have fair access to technical education and training facilities. This is an important way of removing one of the primary sources of inequity and poverty and providing everyone with a chance to push ahead on the basis of his innate ability and the training he has acquired.

Access to Finance

Lack of access of the poor to finance is undoubtedly the most crucial factor in the failure to bring about a broad-based ownership of businesses and industries and thereby realise the egalitarian objectives of Islam. Unless effective measures are taken to remove this drawback, a better and widespread educational system will only help raise efficiency and incomes but be ineffective in substantially reducing the inequalities of wealth. This would render meaningless the talk of creating an egalitarian Islamic society. Fortunately, Islam has a clear advantage here over both capitalism and socialism on account of a financial system which is built into its value system and which provides biting power to its objective of socio-economic justice. This will be discussed later.

2. REDUCING CONCENTRATION IN OWNERSHIP

The most serious impediment to development with justice is the existing concentration in ownership of means of production in Muslim countries, as it is in all market economy countries. Unless this situation is changed through the adoption of certain radical measures permissible within the framework of the *Shari'ah*, it may not be possible to make a perceptible progress in realising the egalitarian goals of Islam. The Islamic strategy in this case is in sharp contrast with that of socialism which, in order to remove the distributional injustice of capitalism, reduced human beings to a permanent state of wage slavery and also killed their initiative and spirit of enterprise by collectivisation of all means of production and centralisation of decision-making.

Proliferation of ownership and decentralisation of decision-making appear to be more in conformity with the dignity and freedom that are associated with the status of *khalīfah*, bestowed upon human beings by God. This proliferation must be brought about in both the rural and the urban areas and in agriculture as well as in industry and commerce through land reforms and rural development; proliferation of small and microenterprises (SMEs); broad-based ownership and control of corporations; revival of the Islamic teachings about *zakāh* and inheritance; and reorganisation of the financial system in the light of Islamic teachings.

LAND REFORMS AND RURAL DEVELOPMENT

A predominant proportion of the population in most Muslim countries is dependent on agriculture for income, employment and general well-being. However, a constellation of historical and political forces has led to a socio-economic structure that is inherently unjust and perpetrates exploitation and misery of the rural population. Nevertheless, in official policies this sector has failed to receive the priority it deserves for removing the prevailing inequities and inefficiencies. Unless measures are adopted to make the agricultural sector more efficient and equitable, the poorer Muslim countries will find it difficult to remove poverty and inequalities or to accelerate development.

A small number of absentee landlords controls large tracts of land in rural areas and a substantial part of the farming population is either landless or has uneconomic holdings. This sets the stage for exploitation by both the landlord and the money-lender and serves as one of the major sources of persistent economic inequalities and absence of democratic processes. The poverty of tenant-farmers and rural labourers prevents them from adopting better farming techniques, thus freezing them into a state of permanent poverty and deprivation. It also kills the incentive of the rural population to put in their best and creates in them the characteristics of indolence, dishonesty and apathy. Moreover, it also drives the rural population to urban areas in search of work, where they face unhealthy living conditions and separation from their loved ones. Thus social control weakens and, combined with low wages and other frustrations, contributes to rise in crime and social unrest.

It is not possible to uplift the socio-economic condition of the rural masses or to strengthen the roots of democratic institutions in Muslim countries without making land reforms the cornerstone of all economic policies. Land reforms, however, hover around the size of landholdings and the terms of tenancy. Unless both of these are settled in conformity with the demands of socio-economic justice, it will be difficult to make a significant headway in realising the *maqāṣid*.

Size of Landholdings

If land had been acquired through fair means and cultivated either by the owner himself or leased to tenant farmers on just terms, and if the Islamic system of inheritance had also been faithfully applied, landholdings would not have become concentrated in the hands of a few families. However, since land has been acquired for centuries through unfair means in many parts of the Muslim world and the Islamic law of inheritance has been disregarded, landholdings have become inequitably distributed, subjecting most of the rural population to lives of virtual slavery, poverty and misery. Given this highly unjust situation, it is important to set a ceiling on the maximum size of landholdings and to distribute the surplus equitably among landless peasants.

The *Sharī'ah* does not visualise the setting of such limits on private wealth in normal circumstances.[4] Nevertheless, the *Sharī'ah* does authorise the state to take all measures that are necessary for realising the *maqāṣid*, provided that they are not specifically prohibited by the *Sharī'ah*.

Since land ownership is concentrated in the lands of a few families, the existing exploitation, poverty, and inefficient use of land and labour will continue, and the goal of realising an equitable distribution of wealth will remain permanently frustrated as long as the combined monopolistic and monoposmatic power of landlords is not broken by imposing certain reasonable limits on the maximum size of land held by one family. Even the enormity of the present rural population relative to the limited size of total available land necessitates the adoption of such a measure for the realisation of the *maqāṣid*.

A number of renowned scholars have, therefore, argued in favour of such limits to restore an equitable balance in ownership and to safeguard the social interest.[5]   Since the *Sharī'ah* requires the payment of 'just' compensation to 'rightful' owners, the land need not be given away to the peasants free. It should, rather, be given at a fair price, the entire value being realised by the government gradually over a number of years out of the peasants' earnings, and used partly to compensate the 'rightful' (and only the 'rightful') owners and partly to meet some of the costs of rural development.

Terms of Tenancy

In addition to reducing the size of landholdings it is also important to reform the terms of tenancy. While the objective of establishing justice between the landlord and the tenant remains undisputed by the *fuqahā'* of all schools of Muslim jurisprudence, the nature of land tenancy has been one of the most controversial issues in *fiqh* literature.[6]   A small minority of the jurists permits neither share-cropping nor fixed-rent tenancy, and requires that the land-owner should cultivate himself whatever land he can and grant the use of the balance to someone who can do so.[7] A larger minority of the jurists allows share-cropping but prohibits fixed-rent tenancy.[8]   Their contention is that although initially the Prophet, may the peace and blessings of God be on him, discouraged both share-cropping and fixed-rent tenancy, later on he allowed share-cropping, and this became a widespread practice among the Prophet's Companions and their Successors.

A predominant majority of the jurists, however, allows both share-cropping and fixed-rent tenancy, this being consistent with the permissibility of both *mudārabah* and leasing in the *Sharī'ah*. Their rationale is that the poverty of most Muslims in the early Madinan period had led the Prophet, may the peace and blessings of God be on him, to discourage both share-cropping and fixed-rent tenancy. However, later on when the economic conditions of the Muslims improved, he allowed both, and not just share-cropping, as is argued by the second group.[9]

Nevertheless, a number of jurists feel that, even though fixed-rent tenancy is allowed, it is *makrūh* (undesirable).[10] According to them share-cropping is preferable because, by requiring both the land-owner and the tenant to share in the reward as well as the risk of farming, it is closer to the Islamic concept of justice, in contrast with fixed-rent tenancy, which assures the landlord a fixed return even though the tenant may or may not be able to have any output.

To be fair to the jurists who allow fixed-rent tenancy, they have tried to ensure justice to the tenant by laying down a number of conditions for the validity of a land-lease contract. For example, according to Imām Mālik, if the output gets destroyed or the lessee is unable to cultivate the leased land due to circumstances beyond his control (e.g. flood or draught), then the lease contract becomes voidable because of excessive risk and uncertainty (*gharar*).[11] In spite of this controversy, a number of jurists find it within the competence of an Islamic state to prohibit fixed-rent tenancy, at least temporarily, or to regulate it sufficiently, if this is necessary for realising the egalitarian goals of Islam.[12]

Since tenants and landless farmers are weak and powerless and, for sometime, are likely to remain so in spite of the enforcement of a limit on the size of landholdings, fixed-rent leasing of land may continue to be a source of injustice and poverty when rents are high and output continues to be uncertain.

It would hence be desirable for Muslim governments to make share-cropping the general basis of land lease and to strive for a just sharing of the output between the landlord and the tenant. This should continue at least until the power base in rural areas has become sufficiently broadened and the exploitative edge of landholding families has been substantially blunted. The radical practice instituted by the Prophet, may the peace and blessings of God be on him, in the early Madinan period indicates that the Islamic state has the authority to undertake all measures considered necessary for improving the well-being of the peasants and landless farmers and for reducing concentration of wealth in the Muslim society.

Rationale and Objections

The importance of land reforms for creating the egalitarian and democratic climate that Islam visualises cannot be overstated. Distribution of land is a major determinant of the distribution of income and the incidence of poverty.[13] The role of land reforms in the relatively more equitable development of Japan, Taiwan and South Korea has already been discussed in chapter 3. Even other countries, which have combined economic growth with an equitable distribution of landholdings, have been able to achieve a relatively more equitable distribution of income, while those which have allowed the concentration of landholdings to continue are suffering from a higher incidence of poverty and a more inequitable distribution of income.[14]

The creation of a rural sector of small, independent proprietary farmers would help provide a great boost to farmer incentives in Muslim countries, thus raising agricultural output and accelerating development. Combined with the proliferation of SMEs, it would help reduce the migration of farm population to urban areas and the associated urban congestion, crime and violence. The reduction of inequalities of income and wealth would also tend to strengthen democratic processes in these countries.

Given the flagrant inequities that now exist, land reform is not an option which the governments may or may not consider seriously. If a meaningful land reform is not implemented, it will come ultimately through a violent revolution. Historical experience shows that when such revolutions take place, all ethical values get trampled. Landlords may in this case lose not only their lands through expropriation but also their lives and other belongings. It would hence be in their own larger, long-run interest to strive voluntarily for a just land reform.

It is argued by some that land reforms may tend to make agriculture inefficient by reducing the size of landholdings. Such a contention is not upheld by a number of empirical studies conducted in different countries. These studies have confirmed that farm size and output per acre are inversely correlated.

This implies that small farms are more efficient than large farms.[15] Empirical evidence that is in conflict with this view, has been explained by the tendency of resources (such as better seeds, credit, water supply and fertilizer) to gravitate towards large farms as a result of the ability of big landlords to use their wealth as a collateral to borrow from financial institutions.[16] Even according to the World Bank, "the resilience and productivity of small family farms throughout the world is striking", specially in view of the considerable disadvantages faced by them in terms of limited access to services, markets and productive inputs such as fertilisers.[17] It is important to bear in mind that implementation of land reforms does not necessarily imply that landholdings be reduced below a certain economically viable level.

Rural Development

Land reforms, though indispensable for reducing concentration of wealth, will not by themselves take the Muslim countries very far in realising the *maqāṣid* unless there is a simultaneous effort to remove some of the other disadvantages from which the entire agricultural sector is suffering — disadvantages that reduce efficiency and output in the agricultural sector, aggravate rural unemployment, depress rural incomes, and accentuate inequalities.

The most serious disadvantage is the absence of external economies of an efficient infrastructure (roads, schools, electricity and health facilities) due to neglect of the agricultural sector in government budgetary appropriations. Unlike the rich industrial countries, which encourage farmers through various incentives including protection from imports, most developing countries discriminate against their farming sector.[18] They try to offset the inflationary impact of government budgetary deficits through overvalued exchange rates and low administered food prices.

Such policies have turned the terms of trade against agriculture and SMEs, lowered agricultural output, increased dependence on imports, reduced the exports and depressed rural incomes. The depressed rural incomes, combined with the inequitable land tenure system, do not leave an adequate surplus to enable tenant-farmers to undertake the necessary investments in agriculture and SMEs. This accentuates rural unemployment and under-employment.

There is thus a vicious circle of poverty, paucity of investments, lower output and unemployment. The pressure of population in urban areas has also consequently risen, leading to a decline in urban wages and the creation of slums with miserable living conditions. Hence, the hub of the problem in rural areas, as the authors of *Poverty and Hunger*[19] have indicated, is income distribution rather than agricultural technique.

Another serious disadvantage faced by the agricultural sector is the lack of availability of financing to small farmers and micro enterprises. "Constant indebtedness to traders, informal money lenders, loan sharks or relatives, perpetuates the poverty of poor people."[20] The result is that small farmers do not have the financing to purchase better quality agricultural inputs and to operate micro enterprises to raise their incomes and to keep themselves fully occupied.

Hence an equitable distribution of landholdings would by itself not lead very far unless suitable arrangements are also made to provide adequate financing not only to finance agriculture but also to small enterprises in rural areas so that the farmers have an additional source of employment and income and their economic condition improves.[21] This should naturally be done within the framework of the alternative to interest-based system that can be developed in consonance with the values and teachings of Islam.[22] This may be impossible to achieve unless the governments and commercial banks which have subsidised large urban enterprises for decades through concessionary or prime-rate financing now tilt the balance in favour of agriculture. How can this be done will be discussed later.

Land reforms supported by other measures to liberate the peasants from the inequities and deficiencies they are suffering from, should not only help considerably expand the productivity of the agricultural sector but also dim the attraction of the bright lights of the city, thus helping reverse the shift of population from rural to urban areas and lowering urban congestion and crime. It would, nevertheless, be necessary to bring about a change in the attitude and work habits in rural areas. This may be attained more speedily and effectively if social change is inspired by Islam. The mosques already play an important role in rural life and their proper use could open up an effective way of inculcating the desired characteristics in the rural population.

PROLIFERATION OF SMALL AND MICRO ENTERPRISES (SMEs)

The counterpart of rural land reforms in the industrial and business sectors is the proliferation of efficient SMEs in rural as well as urban areas. This would complement land reforms in reducing the prevailing concentration of wealth and power in Muslim countries. It also has other advantages which occupy a place of high priority in the Islamic value frame.

The proliferation of SMEs would be in sharp contrast with the prevailing situation in the capitalist and socialist worlds. Large businesses dominate the economic and political scene in capitalist countries and the long-term trend seems to be in favour of even bigger businesses and farms. Consequently, competition, which was the predominant form of market relations in the nineteenth century in the capitalist world, has ceased to occupy that position.[23]

To solve this problem, socialism brought about state ownership of all means of production. This has increased wage slavery and intensified alienation. It has also eliminated competition and reduced incentive and efficiency. It is not yet clear what trend the move towards privatisation of socialist large enterprises will reflect with respect to their size.

While there may be nothing basically wrong in large enterprises if they are more efficient and do not lead to concentration of wealth and power, it seems that the adoption of a policy of generally discouraging large enterprises except where they are inevitable, and of encouraging SMEs, as much as possible, would be more conducive to the realisation of *maqāṣid* in Muslim countries.

This will have a number of advantages besides reducing concentration of wealth and power. It will be more conducive to social health because ownership of business tends to increase the owner's sense of independence, dignity and self-respect. It will induce such owners to innovate and to work harder for the success of their own business. It will create a healthier environment for competition and thus contribute to greater efficiency. It will also help expand employment opportunities at a faster rate, as will be discussed later in this chapter.

WIDER OWNERSHIP AND CONTROL OF CORPORATIONS

Since SMEs may not be feasible for all types of economic activity, it may be preferable to choose the corporate form of business organisation for large enterprises wherever they are necessary. This has the potential of making a positive contribution towards the proliferation of ownership. However, the corporation as it exists in the West is a primary source of concentration of wealth and power.[24] Even though corporations constitute the dominant sector of the economy and exercise an immense power to make basic product, price and investment decisions that affect the entire nation and, in fact, the world,[25] they do not reflect the political democracy of the West in their decision-making.[26] Corporations operate as autocratic institutions; the holding of controlling stock by a few families makes it possible for them to have control over all policies.[27]

This is the natural consequence of the Western interest-based financial system, which makes a high gearing ratio possible and leads to the inverted pyramid of corporate power based on a narrow equity base. The leveraged takeovers witnessed in recent years have made the situation even worse.

The Western corporation does not, therefore, provide a model for Muslim countries. It must be reformed appropriately to reduce the concentration of power. The abolition of interest and a substantial expansion of equity in the capital structure of corporations in accordance with Islamic values will not only minimise the leverage of rich families, but also lead to a wider ownership of corporate shares and a more equitable distribution of power. This may not be enough because most shareholders do not participate in board meetings. Hence, other reforms may also be needed to reduce the sweeping power of directors.

ACTIVATION OF *ZAKĀH* AND ISLAMIC INHERITANCE SYSTEM

The above measures for reducing inequalities of income and wealth would be more successful if they are further strengthened by the activation of the Islamic system of *zakāh* and of inheritance. Unfortunately, even though the implementation of both these systems is an essential part of the obligations of Muslims and indispensable for the realisation of the *maqāṣid*, they have remained dormant for ages.

Zakāh: The Social Self-Help Programme

Islam requires every Muslim, having resources in excess of a certain basic amount, to pay *zakāh* as a given proportion of his or her net worth or agricultural output, for the benefit of mainly the very poor and the destitute. What would be a stronger rationale for making the needed sacrifice to meet one's social obligations than the belief that all resources are a trust from God and must be used for the well-being of all human beings who belong to the one human family of the One God before whom account has to be given about how resources are utilised.

This system of social self-reliance, along with other self-financing arrangements made in modern societies to provide social insurance protection for unemployment, accident, old age and health through deductions from the employees' salary as well as the employers' contributions, should enable the Muslim countries to meet the needs of all without putting the entire burden on the public exchequer as socialism and the welfare state have unwittingly done.

Since it is the obligation of a Muslim to earn his livelihood, it would be desirable to give preference even in *zakāh* disbursements to the objective of enabling the poor to stand on their own feet. *Zakāh* should become a permanent income supplement of only those who cannot be enabled to earn enough through their own effort. This requirement, implemented in a socio-economic environment which encourages SMEs, should make a valuable contribution to the expansion of self-employment opportunities and to the reduction of inequalities.

The levy of *zakāh* on all wealth, including gold and silver and idle balances held in safes, should help induce the *zakāh* payers to seek income on their wealth to enable them to pay the *zakāh* without reducing their wealth. This should help increase the availability of funds for investment. Thus a society where the Islamic values have been internalised, gold and silver holdings and idle balances would tend to go down, leading to a rise in investment and employment.

Inheritance

The distribution of a deceased person's estate in accordance with Islamic injunctions should also help reduce, over time, the skewness in wealth distribution. If necessary, the enforcement of inheritance laws should be carried out in such a way that it does not lead to a rise in unnecessary consumption but rather to an increase in investment and a proliferation in the ownership of means of production.

RESTRUCTURING THE FINANCIAL SYSTEM

The interest-based financial system which the Muslim countries have taken over from the capitalist countries is also one of the primary sources of concentration of wealth and power.[28] Therefore, the Muslim countries may find it difficult to bring about a reduction in inequalities and a proliferation of SMEs unless the entire financial system is restructured in the light of Islamic teachings. This subject will, however, be discussed later.

3. ECONOMIC RESTRUCTURING

The reallocation of resources needed for equitable development is not possible, as indicated earlier, without a thorough economic restructuring that covers all aspects of the economy, including private consumption, government finances, capital formation and production. Some of the relevant aspects of these shall be discussed below.

CHANGING CONSUMER PREFERENCES

Since an accelerated rise in capital formation is indispensable for attaining higher growth and employment, it is necessary to increase savings by squeezing consumption. This objective poses a dilemma. The unequivocal Islamic emphasis on brotherhood and social equality requires that a reduction in consumption be brought about in such a way that the standard of need satisfaction of the poor is not only not worsened but is, in fact, improved.

It is not possible to resolve this dilemma without making a revolutionary change in the prevailing life-styles, particularly of the rich. The inability of the society to fulfil needs is not necessarily the result of a lack of resources but rather of the failure to adopt a consumption pattern which is in conformity with its resources and goals.

Nevertheless, expensive life-styles, which even some of the rich industrial countries can hardly afford, have become a prestige symbol in the otherwise poor Muslim countries. This, along with a number of un-Islamic customs and ceremonies extending from childbirth to marriage and death, has led to an unrealistic consumption pattern which is unwarranted in the light of Islamic teachings and the paucity of resources of most of these countries. The victims of such a life-style are forced to live beyond their means. Aggregate consumption has accordingly risen, savings have lagged behind, and capital formation based on domestic savings remains inadequate. Moreover, since most luxury goods and services carrying a snob appeal are of foreign origin, the pressure on foreign exchange resources has also risen steeply. The resource gap has had to be filled by external borrowing, contributing to a higher debt servicing burden and further squeezing of resources available for investment.

Introducing the Moral Filter

It is not possible to cut down consumption in an equitable manner without distinguishing the 'necessary' from the 'unnecessary' claims on resources. The market system, as discussed earlier, is unable to do this because of its reliance primarily on prices. If the price filter were reinforced by another filter of socially-agreed values, a substantial chunk of aggregate demand could be removed even before it gets expressed in the market. The socialist system, with the absence of even the filter of market-determined price, removes even the secular motivation for efficiency by making resource allocation subject to the whims and vested interests of the politburo members and other power elite.

Needs and Luxuries

What the Muslim countries need to do, therefore, is to distinguish the 'necessary' from the 'unnecessary' by classifying all goods and services into the categories of 'needs' and 'luxuries'. The term 'needs' (including 'comforts') may be used to refer to all those goods and services which fulfil a need or reduce a hardship and thus make a *real* difference in human well-being. The term 'luxuries' may be used to cover all those goods and services which make no real difference in a person's well-being and are wanted mainly for their snob appeal. Everything required for fulfilling needs like capital goods, raw materials, exports, imports, and physical and social infrastructure is 'necessary', while everything that is otherwise, does not fall into this category.

Preparing such a classification may not be a simple job. Islamic values could, however, be helpful. There is an intricate discussion in the *fiqh* literature about necessities (*darūriyyāt*), conveniences (*hājiyyāt*), and refinements (*tahsīniyyāt*). All of these as defined by the *fuqahā'* (jurists), fall within the range of what we have termed 'need' above and do not include luxuries or goods which serve primarily as symbols of high status. Anything that goes beyond 'needs' has been treated by the *fuqahā'* as prodigality and self-indulgence and has been strongly disapproved.[29] This discussion in the *fiqh* literature could be developed further to enable Muslim countries to reduce their prevailing imbalances without compromising their socio-economic goals.

Since Islam is not an ascetic religion, the classification of goods and services into needs and luxuries need not remain constant through space or time. As Islam allows a person to satisfy all his needs and even to go in for all those comforts that would increase his efficiency and well-being, and as the classification of goods and services into the two categories would have to take into account the wealth and general standard of living in a given Muslim country, the perspective about needs is bound to undergo a change over time with the development of technology and the increase in wealth and general standard of living. In fact, most Muslim countries are richer today and can afford a higher standard of need fulfilment than the early Muslim societies.

What is, however, indispensable is the satisfaction of *all* basic needs of *all* human beings in a Muslim society. This goal cannot be realised unless the differences in consumption level which have been allowed in conformity with the status and income of individuals do not go beyond what the economy's resources can bear. They should not reflect snobbery or lead to wide social gaps that can only weaken the bonds of Islamic brotherhood.

The objective should not be to create a monotonous uniformity and drabness in Muslim society. Simplicity can be attained in life-styles without sacrificing creativity and diversity. The criteria for classification into the two categories should hence be the Islamic consumption norms along with the availability of resources and the impact on brotherhood and social equality. Removal of the prevailing imbalances will also have to be an additional criterion as long as these do not become manageable.

Liberalising Need-Fulfilment

'Liberalisation' may hence be construed only within the frame-work of Islamic values related to needs and luxuries. Production, import and distribution of all goods and services falling within the category of 'needs' should be liberalised. Market forces should be allowed to play their full role. The government should do all it can to ensure healthy competition and free interaction between a large number of buyers and sellers. The government should also do all it can to provide the necessary incentives and facilities to increase the supply of need-fulfilling goods and services. Imposition of indirect taxes on the goods and services, deemed necessary, should be at a relatively lower rate and graduated in the reverse order of their priority.

It would, however, be necessary not to liberalise the utilization of resources for luxuries and inessential goods and services to ensure that the imbalances decline and the allocation of resources reflects social and economic priorities. Moral reform could complement the price system by making even the rich to reduce unnecessary consumption voluntarily notwith-standing their purchasing power. However, moral values may remain dormant as they did in the pre-War Japan, Taiwan and South Korea. It is, therefore, necessary to bring about a change in the social mood in the same way as war-related austerity did in these Far Eastern countries.

Without such a change, individuals will conform only under constraint. Two measures could help bring about this change. Firstly, an intensive effort should be made through all the educational media to internalise the Islamic values in the society to such a degree that violation of the Islamic simple-living norm would be considered a social stigma. Since this will take time, it would be desirable to have the campaign for simple living accompanied, at least in the early phase, by a second measure consisting of an officially imposed restriction on luxuries, ostentatious ceremonies, unrealistic doweries, and the display of status symbols.

Even the efforts directed towards reducing corruption are bound to fail unless the governments first strike at one of the major roots of corruption — the ostentatious life-styles now so common in the Muslim countries. Such life-styles almost force the people to resort to unfair means of earning. The acquisitiveness and corruption of many people may tend to decline substantially once they realise that their effort to acquire greater prestige through conspicuous consumption only blemishes their reputation and raises questions about the source of financing.

REFORMING THE PUBLIC FINANCES

Changing consumer preferences in favour of simple living will no doubt reduce private sector pressure on resources and raise the savings needed for investment and development. This will, however, not be enough. Govern-ments in Muslim countries, as in other developing countries, are as blame-worthy as, if not more than, the private sector, for the excessive claims on resources. They have almost lost control over their public finances. The result is that, in spite of high rates of both direct and indirect taxes, they have had to resort to unhealthy levels of budgetary deficits. These deficits have been financed by monetary expansion and excessive levels of domestic and external borrowing. These have generated relatively high levels of inflation and debt-servicing burden which will continue to plague them for a long time.

Priorities in Government Spending

In spite of their excessive spending, the governments have neither laid down the basic infrastructure necessary for balanced and accelerated development nor supplied adequately the services indispensable for realising the egalitarian goals of Islam. Rural infrastructure and agricultural extension services, on which the well-being of a preponderant proportion of the population depends, have been neglected. Education, which should constitute the foundation stone of an Islamic society, has also received inadequate attention. Health expenditure has been concentrated mainly in the major cities, in large capital-intensive hospitals and on curative medicine. Yet the majority of the population lives in the countryside and needs a network of simple clinics and paramedical personnel, control of epidemics and, above all, the provision of clean water supplies, sanitary services and eradication of malnutrition.[30] Housing for the poor has received hardly any public sector attention, and slum areas devoid of public utilities and sanitation have mushroomed. Development of an efficient public transport system has been grossly neglected causing great hardship to the poor who have no transport facilities of their own. Yet much lip service is paid to Islam and its imperative of socio-economic justice.

This sorry state of affairs is bound to perpetuate the existing slow rates of growth and economic inequalities, thus accentuating social tensions and unrest. It is, therefore, necessary for Muslim governments to restructure their spending, so that they are able not only to reduce their overall spending levels but also to reallocate spending to concentrate more on projects that will help accelerate development and realise the socio-economic goals of the *Shari'ah*.

The absence of a serious effort on the part of governments to utilise their limited resources more efficiently is due to a number of reasons. Firstly, there is a lack of realisation that the resources at their disposal are a trust from God. This failing, along with the expensive life-style of government officials, has contributed to corruption. Only a moral reform of the society along with a change in the life-styles of the people, especially those in positions of influence and authority, can remove this shortcoming. Secondly, the absence of an indigenous development philosophy prepared in conformity with the country's own resources and values has led to the absence of well-established priorities. Without the establishment of such priorities it is not possible to set up agreed criteria for judging the 'essential' from the 'inessential' and the 'productive' from the 'wasteful' use of resources. Unless a long-run commitment is made to an Islamic development philosophy, it may not be possible to remove the existing confusion and conflict in policies. Thirdly, the price system has not been used and resources, particularly foreign exchange resources, are acquired or sold by governments and public enterprises at less than their opportunity costs. This contributes to inefficient use of resources. Fourthly, the absence of an elected parliament and a free press deprives the public of a forum for the criticism of government policies. It is hard to conceive that this problem can be solved without establishing a process which would ensure an effective participation of the common man in the government.

Principles of Public Spending

Commitment to Islamic values, and specially to the *maqāṣid*, should help on all four counts. It should, in particular, help reduce the existing arbitrariness in government spending decisions by providing the criteria for establishing priorities. the impact of the *maqāṣid* could be further reinforced by adhering to the following six broad principles adapted from the legal maxims developed over the centuries by Muslim jurists to provide a rational and consistent basis for Islamic jurisprudence.[31]

(1)   The principal criterion for all expenditure allocations should be the well-being of the people (Article 58).

(2)   The removal of hardship and injury must take precedence over the provision of comfort (Articles 17, 19—20 and 30—32).

(3)   The larger interest of the majority should take precedence over the narrower interest of a minority (Article 28).

(4)   A private sacrifice or loss may be inflicted to save a public sacrifice or loss and a greater sacrifice or loss may be averted by imposing a smaller sacrifice or loss (Articles 26—28).

(5)   Whoever receives the benefit must bear the cost (Articles 87—88).

(6)   Something without which an obligation cannot be fulfilled is also obligatory.[32]

These maxims have an important bearing on taxation and government spending in Muslim countries.   To clarify some of their implications for government expenditure programmes, it may be helpful to consider a few examples.

Since general well-being has to be an essential objective of all public spending in accordance with maxim 1, then maxim 6 would require that all physical and social infrastructure projects which help realise this objective through accelerated economic growth, and job creation and need-fulfilment should be given priority over those that do not make such a contribution.

Maxim 2 would require that from among the infrastructure projects which are indispensable, preference should be given to projects that would help remove the hardship and suffering caused, for example, by the prevalence of malnutrition, illiteracy, homelessness and epidemics, and lack of medical facilities, clean water supply and sewerage disposal.

Similarly, the development of an efficient public transport system should acquire priority in accordance with maxim 3   because its absence causes hardship to a majority of the urban population, adversely affecting efficiency and development, and leads to an excessive import of cars and gasoline. While these cars provide extra comfort to a small proportion of the suburban population, a reduction in their imports and diversion of the savings to import of public transport vehicles could be justified on the basis of the maxim. Such a measure would not only reduce the pressure on foreign exchange resources but would also provide comfortable transport services to the majority, with lower congestion and pollution on urban roads.

If priority is to be given to serving the interest of the majority in accordance with maxim 3, then the secondary importance given to rural development programmes has no justification.   Since the majority of the population lives in rural areas and the mass uprooting of people from their families and society causes socio-economic problems, the development of these areas in order to raise agricultural productivity, to expand self-employment and employment opportunities, and to fulfil their needs must take precedence. This will also automatically improve urban life by reducing population congestion.

Inequalities of income and wealth are to be reduced. It becomes indispensable, in accordance with maxim 6, to raise the ability of the poor to earn more through greater and easier access to better educational and training facilities and to finance.

This requires that priority be given to government spending programmes for the establishment of educational and vocational training institutions in rural areas so that everyone who qualifies has an equal access to them. It is also necessary to restructure the financial system to make financing available to a broad spectrum of entrepreneurs in rural as well as urban areas so as to raise self-employment opportunities and to increase the supply of need-satisfying goods and services.

Where to Cut

Given the unhealthy fiscal deficits, the socio-economic goals of Islam cannot be realised without a reallocation of government spending. A decision has hence to be taken about areas where spending must be reduced. Without such a reallocation, either the realisation of the goals will have to be compromised or else spending will exceed the limits of available resources and exacerbate the prevailing macroeconomic and external imbalances. Where can spending be reduced? It is important to identify some of the major areas where savings could be realised.

Corruption, Inefficiency and Waste

The first and the most obvious way to achieve substantial savings is to minimise corruption, inefficiency and waste, which are seriously eroding the ability of Muslim governments to utilise their scarce resources efficiently. According to the Chairman of the Pakistan National Assembly's Public Accounts Committee, "the major part of the development budget is misappropriated". Instances cited by him include: defective buildings collapsing a few years after construction, roads washed away by a single rainstorm, imported railway machinery turning into scrap without being used, imports being sold elsewhere before reaching Pakistan, and big loans extended by nationalised banks to influential people being written off.[33] However, the effort to reduce corruption may have a greater chance of success if it is also accompanied by moral reform, transformation of life-styles and structural changes in the economy.

Subsidies

A second area where substantial savings can be made is subsidies. Even though the welfare of the poor has to be one of the primary considerations of an Islamic state, a number of subsidies provided by Muslim governments (either directly or through public enterprises, and either transparent or opaque) cannot be convincingly supported. Subsidies are usually defended on equity or economic consideration. However, on both these counts they do not stand up to the test of the *maqāṣid* or the Islamic maxims of public spending stated above.

If equity is the goal, the subsidy must redirect income towards the truly needy. It does not. A lower price that does not cover the costs in accordance with maxim 5 tends to benefit the rich more than the poor because of their larger consumption and easier access.[34] This is not defensible in a system committed to socio-economic justice. If value judgements are not an anathema, there is no justification for a lower price or subsidy for the rich or those who can afford to pay. Only those who are unable to pay a realistic price should be helped. Since price discrimination is administratively difficult and since it is desirable to make everyone pay the realistic price, the best way to help the poor is through substantially increased stipends, relief payments and income supplements paid out of appropriations made for this purpose by the government or social service organisations, *zakāh* funds, and other voluntary or compulsory donations.

In this way the government may be able to provide more intensive relief to the needy by using only a proportion of the total amount spent on a general subsidy. The income supplement would give the poor the chance to determine their own priorities and the realistic price would help minimise the wasteful use of goods or services brought about by a general subsidy.

If efficiency is the goal, subsidy must strengthen incentives for the realisation of the *maqāṣid* and allocate resources more effectively. It does not. Agricultural subsidy has mainly helped the big farmers "who have obtained a disproportionate share of it and have used it to amass land and other assets".[35] The subsidy paid to large-scale urban industries on the basis of infant industry argument rarely encourages them to cross the threshold of 'infancy'. However, if the subsidy is used to enable small farmers and SMEs to adopt better technology and inputs, and to stand on their own feet, it could be justified on the basis of the fundamental socio-economic objectives of Islam. But the rural and urban poor "tend to be dispersed, unorganized and politically inarticulate" compared with the urban and rural elite.[36] Hence they rarely get the producers' subsidies of the kind obtained by large-scale industries and influential landlords. The poor nevertheless end up bearing the tax burden of subsidies because the tax systems in these countries are usually regressive.

Public Sector Enterprises

A third important area of saving could be the gradual withdrawal of patronage provided to public sector enterprises as the performance of these enterprises has, by and large, been disappointing in developing countries. They have typically failed to provide the spur to industrialisation and the faster growth that governments had hoped for. Not only have the financial returns often been unimpressive but the social returns have also been poor. This is because they have operated without competition and governments have often placed little emphasis on efficiency and have rarely been prepared to use the sanction of liquidation. Low profitability limits their ability to self-finance their investments. Consequently, they have often been a cause of large budgetary deficits and external debt. In a sample of twenty-seven developing countries in 1976–79, the net budgetary payments to non-financial state owned companies were more than 3 percent of the GDP.[37]

Defence

A fourth area where large savings could be made is defence, because high military spending is the source of substantially large fiscal deficits and of the debt crisis. It complicates stabilisation and adjustment, and adversely affects economic development. Within the framework of Islamic goals and of the principles of public spending discussed above, the claim of national defence for the lion's share in budgetary appropriations loses its rationale in the absence of a serious threat of external aggression.[38]

It is often forgotten that defence spending imposes not only monetary cost but also other costs, including reduced well-being of the poor, leading to social unrest and political instability. Only a few Muslim countries are seriously threatened; most of the others usually make undue fuss about defence on the basis of unrealistic assumptions. Moreover, it is always possible to have better defence with smaller spending if efficiency is ensured in the use of resources; if corruption, which is more rampant in defence than elsewhere, is removed; and if a policy of peaceful coexistence is adopted and unnecessary conflicts with neighbouring countries are avoided.

Since the existence of poverty and extreme inequalities and the absence of adequate educational institutions, hospitals, and public utilities, particularly in rural areas, is subjecting majority of the population to hardship and economic backwardness, there seems to be little moral or economic justification for spending huge sums on defence hardware. The absence of a real threat prevents the government from demanding from themselves and the rich the financial and economic sacrifices that defence requires. Countervailing adjustments are, accordingly, not made in life-styles and government spending, and the needed sacrifice is hence quietly passed on to the urban and rural poor through the low priority given to satisfaction of their needs on the basis of the usual plea of 'lack' of resources.

High defence spending does not even provide the security which the governments claim it does. The 'real' source of security for the poorer Muslim countries lies in internal strength attained through moral reform, economic development and socio-economic justice. No amount of defence spending can provide security against internal disintegration which is gaining momentum in many Muslim countries. It seems that sometimes even the very objective of defence build up, ensuring national and territorial integrity, is jeopardised by 'excessive' defence spending. This is because, as Paul Kennedy has rightly argued, a strong economic base is more vital to a nation, in the long run, than military superiority; and nations which stretch themselves militarily beyond what their economies will sustain are looking for a fall.[39]

One of the most important goals of government policy in Muslim countries should hence be to minimise defence spending through policies of conciliation and peaceful coexistence with a view to release resources for satisfying the needs of the populace. If the Muslim countries concerned take an initiative, there is bound to be public pressure for reduced defence spending even in the neighbouring countries from which the Muslim countries feel the psychological threat. Everyone will then be better off. The non-availability of borrowed funds due to the Islamic ban on interest should help compel Muslim governments to resort to conciliatory and peaceful co-existence policies. They also need to derive inspiration from the Prophet, peace and blessings of God be on him, who signed a truce agreement with the Makkans on extremely unfavourable terms to secure a period of peace and tranquillity.

Tax Reform

While spending needs to be reduced and reallocated, the tax system, which is as guilty of fiscal mismanagement as expenditure policies, also needs to be reformed in the interest of greater equity and higher revenue. Muslim countries, like other developing countries, are not so much over-taxed as they are badly taxed. The tax base is narrow and so the tax rates are high. Tax base, tax rates and corruption are parts of a vicious circles. The narrower the tax base, the higher must be the rate to achieve a given amount of revenue. The higher the tax rate, the greater is the incentive for corruption. This vicious circle leads not only to economic distortions but also to a greater reliance on indirect taxes. It is a well known fact that "tax evasion by the well-to-do is colossal, and they are anyhow relatively very few, while the poor are many. Taxation becomes forced to rely on regressive indirect taxes."[40] The reform of the entire tax system and the collecting machinery are hence indispensable.

Restrained Deficits

Muslim countries have no alternative to expenditure and tax reform. Increased reliance on monetary expansion, borrowing and foreign aid is not feasible. Monetary expansion contributes to inflation. The rate of inflation in low- and middle-income Muslim countries was 23.8 percent in 1989. Although this rate was lower than that of 78.8 percent in all developing countries, it was substantially higher than that of 4.5 percent in industrial countries which are their major trading partners.[41]

This difference in the rates of inflation between the Muslim and the industrial countries has led to a steep decline in the external value of their currencies and created a serious dilemma for them. If their governments devalue their currencies officially to reflect the domestic role of inflation, their rate of inflation accelerates further and accentuates the difficulties of the poor, thus creating political problems for the governments. On the other hand, if they try to avoid a realistic devaluation, their exports become uncompetitive in the international market and increase their dependence on borrowing and aid.

Borrowing does not bear a great promise because the debt-service burden of both domestic and foreign debts of these countries has already risen to an intolerably high level. The external debt of low- and middle-income Muslim countries rose at the rate of 9.8 percent per annum during the decade from 1980 to 1989 when their gross national product and their exports of goods and services rose at the substantially lower rates of 1.8 percent and 6.3 percent per annum respectively. Their debt-servicing burden rose at the rate of 9.3 percent per annum.[42]

The prospects for receiving increasing doses of foreign aid are also not very bright. After the failure of communism, the strategic importance of Muslim countries has definitely gone down. Moreover, the expected increase in the transfer of resources to communist countries to help them in their economic reform will also adversely affect the flow of aid to Muslim countries.

Muslim countries should consider this change in their international geo-political environment as a blessing in disguise and restructure their economies in such a way that their dependence on aid declines. They should make every effort to use effectively whatever aid they are able to get to accelerate development with justice and to minimise its use for private luxury consumption and unproductive public sector spending. The Prophet's *hadīth* saying that: "The hand that is above is better than the hand that is below",[43] should be no less applicable to nations than it is to individuals.

Financing Deficits Islamically

The Islamic injunction against interest should prove to be of great help in realising greater efficiency in public sector spending. Since interest-based borrowing may be permissible only in emergencies or extremely difficult circumstances, governments will have to raise their tax revenues to be able to finance their current and unproductive outlays.

Since there is a limit to the extent to which tax revenues may be raised, governments will not be able to overstretch themselves. They will be forced to keep their wasteful and unnecessary current expenditures under control and to apply cost-recovery methods in the pricing of goods and services supplied by them.

The governments may also have to resort increasingly to leasing of infrastructure projects, financed and implemented by the private sector on a competitive basis in accordance with government specifications. They may have to invite private sector participation in the equity of projects which are commercially viable, but the implementation of which is not desired to be left to the private sector for some overwhelming reason. They may also find it necessary to encourage private philanthropists to construct and run, as many as possible, educational institutions, hospitals, housing schemes for the poor, orphanages and other social service projects by taking effective measures to revive the institution of *awqāf* (charitable trusts) which have played an important role over a greater part of Muslim history.

Since borrowing does not obviate, but rather only postpones, the ultimate need for sacrifice, the ban on interest should prove to be a blessing by removing the long-run heavy debt-servicing burden it normally entails. The constraint it will impose on government spending in the short-run may tend to be more than offset by the healthy discipline it will impose on the governments, the sustained, steadier growth it will generate in the economy, the greater cooperation it will bring about between the governments and the private sector, and the much smaller debt-servicing burden it will create in both the domestic and external sectors of the economy.

To avoid an excessive squeeze in the initial stage, the governments may apply the prohibition gradually and not in one stroke. An unscrupulous government may try to find the easy way out by borrowing excessively from the central bank. This would hurt the Islamic imperative of making money a reliable measure of value through price stability. Accordingly, it would be unrealistic for a Muslim government to talk of Islamisation without making a serious effort to reduce its budgetary deficits.

RESTRUCTURING THE INVESTMENT CLIMATE

Implementation of Islamic consumption norms should also help increase savings. But savings may not necessarily get diverted to capital formation, and even if they do, just a rise in capital formation is not the apex of achievement. What is needed is capital formation that would lead to need fulfilment, export expansion and a rapid rise in self-employment and employment opportunities. Therefore, it is not enough to cut consumption; it is also necessary to foster a suitable investment climate.

In the present-day Muslim societies, a substantial part of even the existing low-level of savings goes into unproductive channels like hoardings (gold, precious stones and jewellery) and capital flight. Capital flight has become a serious problem for most developing countries. During the eleven years from 1974 to 1985, about $150—200 billion of the total capital outflow of $250 billion from capital importing countries, represented capital flight.[44]

Capital flight of this magnitude depresses domestic investment and makes sustained growth more difficult to achieve. If the same policies continue, it would be difficult to prevent capital flight and to raise domestic investment, thus frustrating the realisation of the socio-economic objectives of Islam.

In keeping with the already-quoted maxim: "Something without which an obligation cannot be discharged is also obligatory", productive investment of one's savings to help bring about need fulfilment and increased self-employment or employment is the religious obligation of all Muslims who are capable of saving.

This obligation becomes even more compulsive when we realise that the Prophet, peace and blessings of God be on him, himself glorified productive effort and investment by saying: "If a Muslim plants a tree or cultivates a field such that a bird or a human being or an animal eats from it, this deed will be counted as an act of charity."[45] The Prophet, peace and blessings of God be on him, also discouraged disinvestment by saying: "He who sells a house [without need], but does not invest the proceeds in something similar, God will not bless the proceeds."[46] Caliph 'Umar used to say: "He who has wealth, let him improve [develop] it and he who has land, let him cultivate it."[47]

Given these values, it should be possible to make productive investment take the place of conspicuous consumption as a prestige symbol in a Muslim society such that the benefits that others can derive from savings are actualised. The levy of *zakāh* on all net worth, including currency hoardings and gold and silver jewellery, should prove to be of great help in inducing savers to get into income-earning financial or real assets to be able to offset the impact of *zakāh* on their savings.

Removing the Hurdles

However, even these values may, by themselves, fail to promote productive investment. People tend not to commit funds for long-term productive investments unless there is a proper investment climate. Some of the factors which vitiate the investment climate are the absence of an adequate social and physical infrastructure, an unjust tax system, political uncertainties, continuous depreciation in the exchange rate of the country's currency, and an arsenal of unwarranted controls. A reference has already been made to the need for infra-structure construction and tax reform. The remaining three factors are briefly discussed below.

Political Uncertainties

There is no immediate solution to political uncertainties which are the result of poverty, socio-political unrest, and absence of democratic processes. These have been further aggravated by shifting loyalties of the ruling elite to capitalism, socialism and Islam in response to the conflicting demands of their own vested interest, international power politics and the people's aspirations. This has generated confusion and contributed to an absence of a firm direction in policies and strategies. Making a serious commitment to Islam and allowing democratic processes to play their full political role should help provide the needed direction and stability of policies.

The *Sharī'ah* clearly defines the rights and limitations of property-holders and the legal enforcement of these should help remove the fears of investors about arbitrary seizures and nationalisation. In his address, delivered on the occasion of his Farewell Pilgrimage, the Prophet, peace and blessings of God be on him, declared: "Your lives and your properties are as sacred as this day of the *Hajj*."[48] Accordingly, the jurists have unanimously ruled against arbitrary confiscation and nationalisation of property by the state. Abū Yūsuf epitomised this ruling in the legal maxim: "The ruler has no right to expropriate anything except by a clear and established right."[49] Even if there is need for nationalisation or public use of private property, the *Sharī'ah* requires a just compensation in conformity with the legal maxim: "A public need does not invalidate a private right."[50]

The clear verdicts of the *Shari'ah* should become reflected in the legal framework of all Muslim countries. They should define clearly and stipulate legally all those sectors of the economy where only public enterprises may be permissible and sectors where private enterprise will be free to play its role. Such a classification should be further re-inforced by a legal guarantee in favour of just compensation in case of re-classification.

The number of public enterprises will have to be kept at a minimum anyway because of the prohibition against interest and the inability of the governments to raise sufficient financing for such enterprises through taxes or sale of shares. Once such guarantees have become integrated into the country's Constitution and legal framework and it is realised that their fountainhead is the *Shari'ah*, it would be difficult for any government to disregard them in the interest of its own domestic popularity and international standing.

Exchange Controls and Currency Depreciation

The continuing depreciation of the currencies of most Muslim countries cannot be prevented without reducing claims on resources, particularly foreign exchange resources through the restructuring of private and public sector spending in the manner already discussed. Instead, most Muslim governments rely on exchange controls (overvalued exchange rates with import licensing), high tariffs, and promotion of import-competing industries.

Exchange controls, as evidence has indicated, have been largely ineffective.[51] They lead to the creation of a dual market of official and black market exchange rates. The overvalued official rate encourages imports and discourages exports, thus worsening the allocation of resources and depressing the rate of economic growth. They contribute to socio-economic injustice by subsidising recipients of import licences at the expense of consumers and exporters; the consumers continue to pay for imports at the opportunity cost of foreign exchange while the exporters receive less for their output. They also promote corruption and inefficiency.

The various bonus schemes adopted to promote exports in the absence of a realistic exchange rate succeed only in exacerbating injustice and corruption. The benefit of these schemes does not permeate to the actual producers; their resources do not consequently increase to enable them to acquire improved inputs and better technology. Their productivity hence continues to remain low.

Tariffs and Import Substitution

Higher tariffs, unlike realistic exchange rates, constitute a single-edged weapon. If applied effectively, they can discourage imports, but do not encourage exports. However, when high tariffs are used in developing countries with weak customs administration, and without any attempt to change the social mood, there is under-invoicing, smuggling and tariff evasion. This raises the relative profitability of highly taxed, but smuggled, luxury goods and distorts resource allocation against need satisfaction. Hence a more effective strategy would be to ban the import as well as the display of luxury goods.

Promotion of import-competing industries is no doubt necessary to reduce the pressure on foreign exchange resources and to promote employment and growth. However, in the absence of a consistent development philosophy, the selection of import-competing industries is arbitrary with no relationship to the promotion of development with justice or the rational principles of resource allocation.

Such arbitrarily selected industries receive maximum government patronage in the form of subsidised financing, high tariff protection, exemption from duties on the import of capital goods and raw materials, and tax holidays. These industries usually tend to be large-scale and are established in urban areas. Since most of them are capital-intensive and use a more sophisticated technology, their contribution to employment is not as much as that of labour-intensive SMEs.

The high tariffs imposed to protect these industries contribute not only to higher prices for consumers but also, along with other privileges, to the unearned enrichment of those who receive licences for such industries and resort to under-invoicing. More and more of the nation's resources accordingly move into such industries distorting resources allocation against need-fulfilment and enriching the urban and rural rich. Furthermore, in highly protected industries there is usually little competition.[52]

Agriculture and SMEs, which should really be the candidates for protection because of their great potential for growth, need-fulfilment and employment creation, are neglected. They suffer from lack of government support, overvalued exchange rates, import subsidies and commodity aid.

Since most units operating in these sectors are small, unorganised and inarticulate, they are unable to exert any political pressure. Concentration of landholding and absence of democratic processes worsens their position even further. The result is the vicious circle of neglect and poverty of these sectors and their inability to finance investments in improved technology. This is undoubtedly in conflict with the basic socio-economic objectives of Islam.

Bureaucratic Controls

Probably the greatest obstacle to investment in Muslim countries, as in other developing countries, is the bureaucratic red-tape. This springs from the heavy reliance of governments on controls to realise their objectives, rather than on moral reform and the creation of a proper enabling environment. Controls lead to waste of time of investors and an unnecessary rise in costs. Unless most of these controls are dismantled, it would be difficult to improve the investment climate even if savings increase.

The general spirit of Islamic teachings is freedom of enterprise within the value-frame of Islam. Controls are an inevitable source of corruption and even the reform and improvement of morals under the influence of Islamic teachings might not be able to prevent officials from succumbing to temptation. There is, moreover, no justification for controls on the local manufacture or import of need-fulfilling consumer goods and the raw materials and capital goods needed for their manufacture.

Foreign Equity Capital

The Islamic ban on interest will make it indispensable for Muslim countries to encourage and facilitate foreign equity investment. This should no doubt be desirable because "equity investment has proved to be beneficial to developing countries", and it should be possible to attract it by creating a favourable climate for it.[53]

It would be difficult to defend stipulations against foreign equity investment which does not conflict with the Islamic values and might even help realise some of the basic socio-economic objectives of Islam. It also has the advantage that it makes available foreign exchange as well as technology and management which are scarce factors in Muslim countries and are needed to raise productivity. It does lead to foreign exchange outflow at a later stage. but only if the investment earns a positive return. Thus, in contrast with borrowing, the risk is shared with the foreign investor instead of being borne entirely by the host country.

The favourable climate that readjustment of economic policies in the light of Islamic teachings will create, should itself constitute a positive factor in attracting foreign equity capital, and no extra measures may need to be adopted. The Islamic emphasis on the fulfilment of all contractual obligations, if articulated legally, should help provide the reassurance that foreign investors need. The removal of exchange controls on all current account transactions falling within the Islamic value frame, including the ease of profit remittances, is what Islam would find desirable under normal peacetime conditions.

It would also be necessary to provide assurances about capital repatriation. But how could an Islamic state even consider the idea of preventing an expatriate investor from getting his right as long as repatriation is in accordance with agreed terms and conditions? According to the World Bank: "Countries that have followed a more open development strategy have had fewer problems with direct investment."[54] However, until such time as the Muslim countries are able to attract more foreign equity investment, it may be unavoidable for them to tolerate conventional borrowing to the extent absolutely necessary to finance productive, self-liquidating projects that are truly needed for realising the *maqāṣid*.[55]

NEED-BASED PRODUCTION

Restructuring the investment climate can only help increase the volume of investments. It is necessary to adopt measures to ensure that this increase in investment does not get diverted to the production of luxury goods and services, but goes rather to the production of need-fulfilling and exportable goods and services and the capital goods and raw materials needed for this purpose.

No effort should be made to accomplish this objective by means of controls; this would not succeed. The more preferable and effective strategy would be to change individual preferences, remove obstacles, and provide incentives and facilities for making long-term commitment of funds. All privileges and subsidies, explicit or implicit, which provide an edge to the production and import of luxuries and status symbols must be withdrawn. Emphasis of government fiscal, monetary and commercial policies should also be tilted in favour of need fulfilment, exports and capital formation.

The general tendency to resort to price controls on necessities leads to long-run shortages in their supply by reducing their profitability and, hence, discouraging investment in their production. This becomes a permanent source of injury to the poor. In contrast, the long-run supply of luxury items arises, thus serving the interests of the well-to-do.

Hence the *Shari'ah* has not permitted price controls under normal circumstances when there is not a national emergency (war or famine) or when businesses are not creating an artificial shortage through monopoly, collusion or hoarding. The short-term harm that the removal of price controls on necessities will inflict on the poor should be undone through the adoption of a gradual approach and the use of transfer payments and other measures discussed in this book.

The support to agriculture and rural development and to SMEs, as discussed later, will play an important role in encouraging need-fulfilment and exports. The restructuring of the banking system along with Islamic lines should also be an essential element of the whole reform programme.

A NEW DEAL FOR THE UNEMPLOYED AND THE UNDEREMPLOYED

One of the most constructive ways of accelerating growth with justice is to enable every individual in society to use his or her creative and artistic abilities efficiently and productively to the fullest extent. This goal cannot be materialised if the prevailing high levels of involuntary unemployment and underemployment continue. The main policy instruments usually adopted to reduce unemployment and underemployment are expansion of aggregate demand and establishment of capital-intensive large- and medium-scale urban industries.

Promoting SMEs

While the conventional policy of aggregate demand expansion is no doubt useful, it is not sufficient and needs to be strengthened by other policies. Within the existing scenario of urban bias of government policies, flagrant inequalities of income and wealth, and the demonstration effect of western life-style, reliance on demand expansion helps mainly the rich and spills over to a substantial degree into imports of goods and services for conspicuous consumption. Consequently, its full benefit does not go to the indigenous craftsmen and artisans. The demand for their products does not rise significantly and the goal of expanding employment hence suffers.

However, if this policy were to be pursued within the perspective of need-fulfilment and promotion of SMEs, the benefit would tend to permeate to a larger proportion of the population. Macroeconomic and external imbalances, which do not make it possible to expand aggregate domestic demand significantly, add further strength to this policy proposal.

Since the poorer Muslim countries have a surplus of labour, scarcity of capital and foreign exchange, and lack the educational infrastructure for training in complex technology, it would be desirable for them to rely more on SMEs than on large- and medium-scale capital-intensive industries if they wish to expand employment and self-employment opportunities. Accordingly, Ḥasan al-Bannā gave cottage industries a prominent place in his discussion of economic reforms in the light of Islamic teachings. These, he stressed, would help provide productive employment to all members of poor families, and thus help reduce unemployment and poverty.[56] Dr. Muhammad Yunus has emphasised another aspect of SMEs by saying: "Wage employment is not a happy road to the reduction of poverty", and that self-employment "has more potential for improving the asset base of an individual than wage employment has."[57]

There is a growing realisation now that "the large-scale 'modern' industrialisation strategies of the previous decade generally had failed to solve the problems of global underdevelopment and poverty".[58] Studies conducted in a number of countries by the Michigan State University and host-country scholars have clearly indicated the rich contribution that SMEs can make to employment and income. They create new jobs not only directly but also indirectly by expanding incomes as well as demand for goods and services, tools and raw materials, and exports. They are labour-intensive and require less capital and less foreign exchange. They rely primarily on personal savings and retained earnings and need much less access to credit from governments and financial institutions compared with large-scale industries. They invent products, revive lost skills and help economies move into new kinds of work. They can be more widely disbursed and thus help maintain the link between a person's place of work and his home which large-scale industries and hectic urbanisation have severed to the detriment of social health. Moreover, they are at least as efficient as large-scale industries.[59] A Michigan State University study has concluded that they consistently generate more output per unit of capital than do their large-scale counterparts.[60]

Little, Scietovsky and Scott have concluded that "large-scale modern industry is usually much less profitable than the small craft type industries, in addition to being more costly in terms of capital and creating less employment".[61] Some scholars in fact doubt that large-scale industries can be suitable at all under conditions of labour surpluses and capital shortages that are typical of most developing countries.[62] SMEs are hence being widely viewed as "an effective way of fostering the private sector's contribution to both the growth and equity objectives of developing countries".[63]

Even the OECD countries have realised the job-creating potential of small enterprise.[64] Over the last decade they have accounted for a disproportionate share of new jobs, and those industrial countries where they play an important role have had a greater success in achieving lower rates of unemployment.

Hence, a number of these countries have introduced measures to promote them.[65] "No longer are small firms seen as the Cinderella of the business community, rather they are to be courted and encouraged by politicians of all colours."[66] In Italy, artisans, often working in family businesses, are a main factor behind the success of Italian jewellery, gold, silver, leather working, embroidery, glasswork, furniture, pottery, shoemaking, and cloth manufacturing, to mention just a few sectors.[67] In Germany, where the family-owned concern has always played a major part in the economy, there is a renewed awareness of the need to create a favourable climate for small enterprise.[68] Japan's export success is largely due to the vigour of internal competition created by the producing firms through their subcontracting of a lot of work to small businesses on a competitive basis.[69] Small firms are very important in Japan even domestically. They account for fifty percent of Japanese industrial output and seventy-five percent of total Japanese employment.[70] Three-quarters of retail sales are still made in Japan through specialty retailers and small family-run stores which are protected by law.[71] This, along with the widespread use of profit-sharing system, may be among the primary reasons for the lowest rate of unemployment in Japan among industrial countries.[72]

Even in other developed countries where the small firms sector has traditionally been weak, high levels of unemployment have made governments very receptive to their promotion. There has hence been a wealth of public and private sector initiatives to boost the small entrepreneur.

The emphasis of policy in Muslim countries on decentralised production with a proliferation of capital-saving SMEs may perhaps be the most effective way of not only gainfully employing a large part of the rural landless but also the under-occupied members (husband, wife, parents and children) of rural families having a small landholding.

This policy will serve as complementary to agricultural reforms discussed earlier and will support rural development by raising the incomes of rural population and enhancing their ability to purchase better seeds, fertilisers and technology, thus raising even their agriculture output. It will also reduce the outflow of population to urban centres. This will help maintain family solidarity and be more conducive to moral uplift and crime reduction, which are among the important goals of Islam.

While many Muslim countries are critical of the policies of their colonial masters "who systematically destroyed all the fibres and foundations" of their societies, they have done little after independence to revive the skills and crafts that were destroyed.[73] On the contrary, in fact almost all measures have been taken which would lead to stifling SMEs and to patronising large-scale industries and businesses through a high protective wall, liberal import licences, concessionary financing, subsidised inputs and tax holidays.

This is not a judgement against large-scale industry, which will be indispensable in certain sectors of the economy and which should be encouraged and undertaken where necessary, provided that the overall socio-economic benefits exceed the costs and a heavy dose of permanent protection is not needed.

Essential Measures

But how to encourage the proliferation of SMEs in Muslim countries? It requires a number of revolutionary changes in the socio-economic environment. Firstly, there must be a change in life-style away from imported status symbols and in favour of simple domestically-produced products that satisfy needs and utilise more labour. Secondly, there must be a change in official attitudes and policies towards SMEs such that they are not dismissed as inefficient small fry and anachronistic leftovers of the past, but are rather encouraged and helped to realise fully their rich potential. Thirdly, they must be enabled, through help in acquiring better inputs, appropriate technology, effective marketing techniques, and other extension services, to compete in terms of both quality and price with the products of large-scale industries and imports. Fourthly, they must also be enabled to upgrade their skills through better training facilities; this will require a complete overhaul of educational institutions to remove the existing mismatch between the skills in demand and the education offered. Fifthly, they must also be provided access to finance, the lack of which constitutes the most serious obstacle to their development. Finally, it may also be necessary to eliminate, if not to reverse the direction of, the existing bias in favour of large-scale industries which is one of the major impediments to the expansion of SMEs.

The objectives of import-substitution and export promotion may not be realised through the SMEs unless they are helped to acquire more efficient technology to enable them to compete effectively. It would, however, be preferable if such technology is simple, in which case it would have the following advantages. It would require a smaller capital outlay, thus absorbing the growing labour force with a smaller amount of capital. It would minimise the demand for high skills and be thus suitable for Muslim countries with their relatively lower standards of literacy and technical education. It would enable a greater use of locally available materials and reduce the claim on foreign exchange resources. It would be possible to develop and produce it locally, thus helping to reduce the dependence on imported technology. It would also be possible to introduce it in small towns and rural areas, thus reducing regional income disparities and minimising the concentration of population in a few large urban centres, which large-scale enterprise with its capital-intensive and complex technology tends to create. It would thus be what Schumacher calls a "technology with a human face".[74] Even such a simple and inexpensive technology has the potential of leading to a "fairly rapid increase in productivity in underdeveloped countries".[75] It could not only help raise incomes and standards of living but also help achieve redistribution.

4. FINANCIAL RESTRUCTURING

The objective of achieving a proliferation of SMEs in rural and urban areas to solve the major economic problems of unemployment and concentration of wealth would remain only a fond dream unless arrangements are made for their financing. Lack of financing constitutes the most serious drawback in the development of small farms and SMEs. The poor are poor not because of their unwillingness to work hard or lack of skill. They in fact work harder than the rich and have more skill than they can use.

Their main problem is that they do not have access to financial resources necessary for being self-employed, and wage employment either does not utilise their skills optimally or does not pay them adequately to fulfil even their needs, leave alone save for investment. Financing is a powerful political, social and economic weapon and plays a predominant role in determining the power base, social status and economic condition of a person in the modern world. Dr. Muhammad Yunus has hence rightly emphasised that financing for self-employment should "be recognized as a right that plays a critical role in attaining all other human rights".[76] Reform of the financial system should hence constitute one of the key elements of all socio-economic and political reforms.

The Select Committee on Hunger found that "the provision of small amounts of credit to micro enterprises in the informal sector economy of developing countries can significantly raise the living standards of the poor, increase food security and bring about sustainable improvements in local economies". The Committee also concluded that "making credit available to entry level micro entrepreneurs is one way to help end the cycle of poverty and hunger among urban and rural landless poor in developing countries". However, as the Committee indicate, "formal financial institutions in these countries do not recognize the viability of income generating enterprises owned by the poor".[77] Even the Morgan Guarantee Trust Company, the sixth largest bank in the U.S., has admitted that the banking system in developing countries has failed to "finance either maturing smaller companies or venture capitalists", and "though awash with funds, is not encouraged to deliver competitively priced funding to any but the largest, most cash-rich companies".[78]

Since the deposits of commercial banks come from a wide cross-section of the population, it would be rational to consider them as a national resource to be utilised for the well-being of all sectors of the population rather than primarily for the further enrichment of the wealthy and the powerful.[79] This is not possible within the framework of the conventional system in which, as Lester Thurow has rightly observed, credit is granted mainly "to those firms with large internal savings, regardless of whether they are earning above average rates of return on their capital investment".

The result is that "the winners are, as in lottery, lucky rather than smart or meritocratic".[80] The most telling lesson about the conventional banking system comes from Catherine Shaw, a researcher at the London School of Economics' Business History Unit, who says: "The recruitment of business leaders from one social class or a narrow social strata is an ominous symptom. It suggests that society is failing to utilise its total reservoir of ability."[81]

The adoption of a financial system that is inspired by Islamic teachings could be more conducive to the harnessing of this pool of ability and the bringing to a fruition the rich contribution that SMEs can make to output, employment and income distribution. The sharing of risks along with rewards by the financial institutions will substantially reduce the precariousness of a small entrepreneur's position — he will save himself from the back-breaking burden of interest in difficult times by his willingness to pay a higher rate of return in good times. The financial institution is well qualified to share the risk, and could do so without denting its financial strength if it builds loss-offsetting reserves in good times.

However, even if the financial system is reorganized to make it consistent with the teachings of Islam, it would still be necessary to remove two of the primary causes responsible for the failure or inability of commercial banks to finance small farms and SMEs. The first of these is the serious economic disadvantages under which this sector operates, and the second is the great risk and expense to which the commercial banks are exposed.

The first drawback cannot be removed without eliminating the implicit bias in official policies in favour of large-scale urban enterprises and replacing it by a strong commitment to support small farmers and SMEs. The adoption and implementation of the programme, proposed earlier, through appropriate government policies and budgetary support should help gradually divert more and more of commercial bank financing to small farmers and SMEs. The second drawback cannot be removed without reducing the risk and expense of commercial bank lending to such units.

The greater risk of financing SMEs leads to a tough and extensive collateral requirement which they are unable to satisfy. This jeopardises their growth and expansion in spite of their greater potential for contribution to employment, output and income distribution. The financing goes mainly to the rich who are subjected to a lower collateral requirement and which they are able to satisfy without any difficulty because of their greater wealth. Mishan has rightly indicated: "Given that differences in wealth are substantial, it would be irrational for the lender to be willing to lend as much to the impecunious as to the richer members of society, or to lend the same amounts on the same terms of each."[82]

It may be expected that, within the Islamic risk/reward sharing framework, banks may tend to be attracted to provide greater financing to smaller firms because of their well-established greater profitability. Small firms bear a record of better performance in terms of growth in real per capita profits in industrial countries where small entrepreneurs have been encouraged.[83]

Even in developing countries with their extremely difficult environment for SMEs, they have consistently generated, according to a Michigan State University study, more output per unit of capital and are generally more efficient than their large-scale counterparts. Accordingly, the economic profit of smaller firms is consistently larger than that of large firms.[84]

The risk may be reduced by introducing a loan guarantee scheme underwritten partly by the government and partly by the commercial banks.[85] In the case of Islamic banks, the guarantee scheme cannot ensure the repayment of loans with interest as is the case in the conventional system. The scheme would rather cover the 'moral' risk of financing and relieve the bank of the need for collateral from SMEs whose general credentials have been examined and certified by the guarantee scheme. A large number of SMEs would thus be able to get financing from banks without being able to offer the collateral required by the conventional banks. The bank will receive its money back from the guarantee scheme in case of moral failure of the business.

In case of market failure and the resultant loss, the bank should share the consequences with the business in proportion to the financing provided by it. The scheme may also be made to include some other non-commercial risks desired to be covered for increasing the availability of funds to SMEs.

This should not create any apprehensions about the viability of the loan guarantee scheme due to heavy loan losses. As indicated above, the scheme will not bear the entire risk of loan losses. It will bear only the moral risk, the business risk being borne by both the bank and the borrower. Hence, the scheme will not be as heavily burdened with losses as the conventional schemes are. Moreover, the experience of International Fund for Agricultural Development (IFAD) is that credit provided to the most enterprising of the poor is quickly repaid by them from their higher earnings.[86] The Report of the Select Committee on Hunger also indicates that the "micro enterprise projects have recorded significant and impressive loan repayment rates".[87] Testimony from the Grameen Bank in Bangladesh indicates a constant repayment rate of 99 percent since the bank's inception.[88] Other SME credit programmes have yielded similar results. Hence there is no need to be unduly apprehensive about loan losses from such financing.

The additional expense of commercial banks in evaluating and financing SMEs may have to be partly or wholly offset by the government in the interest of the realisation of the basic socio-economic objectives of Islam. Big business has been subsidised by governments for a long time in various ways, including concessionary financing, import licences, overvalued currencies, and subsidised inputs.

To offset this undue advantage received in the past, the governments should now turn the table in favour of small farmers and SMEs. Both the *maqāṣid* and the principles of public spending discussed earlier justify a reasonable allocation of government resources for this purpose. Nevertheless, a part of the increased cost should also be recovered from banks and SMEs, at least for the sake of promoting greater responsibility and efficiency. It may be expected that once the credentials of SMEs have been established and the system has started operating, the costs would tend to go down.

The Islamisation of banks and the financing of SMEs may also help bring into their fold the savings of a large proportion of the rural population not yet absorbed by the banking system because of their lack of trust in conventional interest-based banks and the apathy of banks towards them. This will help mobilise the idle savings in the economy and generate a higher non-inflationary rate of growth. It may also help reduce the attractiveness of gold as a store of value and release savings for investment.

5. STRATEGIC POLICY PLANNING

It will not be possible for Muslim countries to realise the *maqāṣid* within the constraint of their scarce resources unless they take stock of their needs and resources and have a clear understanding of where they are and where they wish to go. It may be possible to do this more effectively if a long-term strategic policy plan is prepared.

Such a plan would enable the state to take a realistic account of all the available physical and human resources and to establish, in the light of this, a set of well-defined priorities. This will help provide a clear direction to government policies and expenditure programmes and initiate effective measures to set in motion the required structural and institutional changes to enable both the government and the private sector to make their full contribution.

The plan should not be comprehensive and dirigiste, trying to achieve, through a maze of regulatory controls, a balancing of all inputs and outputs and their allocation among micro units of the economy. The plan should also not rely on the government being the principal source of investments and enterprise. This is neither feasible nor necessary. Any move in this direction will make the economy less responsive to changing circumstances and stifle individual initiative and enterprise, and so bury it in the contradictions and insoluble problems that afflicted the socialist and developing countries which resorted to such planning. Indeed, these countries have all been forced to move away from such planning.

What is necessary for the Muslim countries to do is to pass all claims on resources through the filter mechanism of Islamic values and to motivate and activate the private sector, through moral and institutional reform as well as economic incentives, to utilise scarce resources with optimum efficiency and equity in order to realise the *maqāṣid*.

The articulation of the Islamic filter mechanism will thus be indispensable. It will help define the goals of the economy in order of priority and specify ways of achieving them. The establishment of priorities within the framework of the *Shari'ah* will help in the analysis of the existing allocation of resources and in pinpointing the direction of change. It will also be necessary to articulate the Islamic values regarding consumption, savings and investment, and work ethics, and to devise educational programmes to promote them. The plan will also have to classify goods and services into needs and luxuries, as discussed earlier.

The public, in general, and the government officials, in particular, will need to be motivated to act in accordance with Islamic values. While belief in accountability before God is essential, it is not sufficient to motivate them to put in their best and to be more efficient. It is also necessary to inculcate simple living and to actualise socio-economic justice. Simple living will reduce the urge for corruption, and the ability to get a due reward for contribution to output will induce workers, entrepreneurs, investors and savers to do their best.

Of course, prices and wages must be normally determined by market forces. However, in the existing situation, with wealth and power concentrated in a few hands, they reflect monopolistic or monopsonistic characteristics and are hence not 'just'. They, therefore, tend to suffocate the drive, initiative, creativity and enterprise of a large proportion of the population. The plan must indicate the policies and institutional reforms needed to remove the existing injustices.

The plan must also specify the structural changes required in the economy to fulfil needs, reduce unemployment and raise the growth rate without creating macroeconomic and external imbalances. The plan must also indicate the institutions that must be established or reformed to reduce substantially the inequalities of income and wealth that now exist, and to bring about a broad-based ownership of businesses and income-earning assets.

The reform of the banking system in the light of Islamic teachings will require the special attention of planners because of the great contribution it can make to efficient and equitable allocation of resources. A thorough reform of the education system is also necessary to make the students better Muslims and more productive. In sum, the plan should not concentrate on any single measure or rely unduly on controls; it should rather use a range of policies and incentives to realise the basic socio-economic objectives of Islam. It should reflect a perceptible change in the development philosophy and strategy.. All policies — fiscal, monetary, incomes, import and production — should be formulated within the framework of this strategic policy plan.

The production, import, distribution and consumption of what fits into the strategic policy plan should be permitted freely through the operation of the price system without bureaucratic controls. Controls, including those on the use of foreign exchange for current account transactions, should be employed only where, and as long as, indispensable.

A general policy of letting social and institutional reform and incentives take the place of controls will help remove inequities in material rewards, harness people's own inner drive for development, and, not only help reduce corruption and attain greater efficiency but, also make innovation and adjustment to changing circumstances easier. However, what does not conform with the plan should not be allowed — irrespective of how rich or resourceful an individual may be. Special consideration should be given to the adverse effect of any policy measure on the poor, and methods should be devised to offset or minimise this.

There should not be changes in policy from quarter to quarter or year to year because the resource perspective, needs and goals of a country do not change that rapidly. Frequent tinkering with policies only generates uncertainties, and enriches mainly those having insider's knowledge. But errors which have been made in the preparation of the plan should be rectified with an open mind and without undue delay. Since the resource endowment of different Muslim countries is different, the same strategic policy of each will somewhat differ from the other in respect of details. What will confer unity on these strategic policies is the fact that all these policies will be oriented to achieving essentially the same set of socio-economic objectives — the *maqāṣid*.

★★★

FIVE

WHY THE FAILURE?

If Islam is capable of providing a workable strategy for development with justice and even to motivate people to fulfil the requirements of such growth, then the question that inevitably arises is: why have the Muslim countries failed to formulate and implement policies in the light of such a strategy? This is a difficult question to answer. A variety of explanations may perhaps be given, pointing out a number of factors — historical, political, economic and sociological — which shed light on the question. In fact, it is hardly possible for us to provide an exhaustive answer to the question, and such an attempt is even beyond the scope of the book. However, we will identify and emphasise one factor — the political factor — which, in our opinion, is one of the most important factors responsible for the failure of the Muslim countries to implement the Islamic strategy for development with justice.

NEED FOR SOUND POLITICAL ORDER

Development with justice is scarcely possible unless the people who are suffering from inequities have a say in the formulation of policies that affect their well-being, unless they participate in the decision-making process and the political system makes it possible for them to exert pressure on the governments for an honest implementation of these policies. As Ḥasan al-Bannā had rightly stressed, governments are the heart of socio-economic reform. If they become corrupt, they may be able to corrupt everything and, if they are reformed, they might reform everything.[1]

Governments, however, can hardly play an effective role in achieving development along with justice unless the common people have an opportunity to freely participate in the political life. Unfortunately, the political realities of the Islamic world fall short of this ideal. The first of the Islamic institutions in the history of Islam to have suffered a compromise was the institution of *khilāfah* (Caliphate) — an institution which reflected the Islamic principles for political life in their ideal form.

The pristine characteristics of Caliphate were gradually replaced by the traditions associated with autocratic and hereditary regimes, which draw little inspiration from the Islamic democratic imperative of *shūrā* (consultation), and which accumulated over time some of the evils associated with such rule.[2] Unless a healthy political system, based on freedom from fear, and providing for participation of people in the decision-making process is established, the Islamic programme for realising the *maqāṣid* may continue to occupy only an ornamental place in the political scheme of things obtaining in the Muslim countries.

CRITERIA FOR A SOUND POLITICAL ORDER

Islam, however, has its own rigorous criteria for a good government. The first of these is that the government is accountable to God, Who is the Sovereign Lawgiver, One Who has the right to lay down the guidelines of man's behaviour. This implies that the government's authority is limited and not absolute. The government is required, in the first place, to abide by the *sharīʿah* and to do all it can to ensure the realisation of the well-being of the people through adoption of all necessary measures, including efficient and equitable use of resources. The Prophet, may the peace and blessings of God be on him, said:

> Everyone of you is a shepherd and everyone is accountable for his flock.[3]

> Anyone who has been given the charge of a people but does not live up to it with sincerity, will not taste even the fragrance of paradise.[4]

> The most beloved of men and the nearest to God in rank on the Day of Judgement will be a just ruler, and the most despised of them and the farthest from Him in rank will be an unjust ruler.[5]

The second criterion of of sound political system is that the rulers should be accountable to the people. This is so because the government is a trust — a trust from God as well as the people — given to those who manage their affairs. The Prophet, peace and blessings of God be on him, clearly emphasised this to Abū Dharr, who wished to acquire a senior government position, "O Abū Dharr! You are weak and this position is a trust. It will be a source of disgrace and regret on the Day of Judgement except for him who acquires it deservedly and fulfils the obligations incumbent on him."[6] Therefore, while the government is accountable to God for its success or failure in living up to the trust, it is also accountable to the people for realising their aspirations in conformity with the terms of the trust.

Human experience shows that governments cannot fulfil their role of realising the aspirations of the people unless they are open to the suggestions and criticism of the common people. Hence, the Prophet, peace and blessings of God be on him, emphasised that one of the demands of faith on Muslims is to render sincere advice to their rulers — an advice that would help them to perform their duties effectively.[7]

But how can people fulfil the obligation of rendering sincere advice to the rulers if there is no freedom of expression and they are not allowed to freely express themselves concerning the policies being pursued by the government? If the rulers do not consider themselves accountable to the people and are unwilling to receive feedback from them regarding government policies, the scope of reform will be greatly reduced. Accordingly, when Abū Bakr became the first Caliph, he categorically emphasised this Islamic imperative in his inaugural address by saying: "If I act rightly, help me, but if I act wrongly, correct me and set me right."[8]

This establishes a two-way flow of rights and obligations. It is the right of the people to participate in the formulation of policies and the obligation of rulers to enable them to do so. It is simultaneously the right of the rulers to solicit help and cooperation from the people if the former try to implement the right policies, and it is the obligation of the people to correct them if they are not doing so.

The above policy statement of Abū Bakr represents the general thinking of the Campanions rather than an isolated opinion of Abū Bakr. This is evident from the fact that 'Umar, the second Caliph, also subscribed to the same principle. When a person tried to prevent someone from criticising him, 'Umar insisted on allowing the person to continue, saying: "There is no good in them if they do not speak out, and there is no good in us if we do not listen to what they say."[9]

Reports about ordinary people criticising the Caliphs, and the Caliphs accepting such criticisms gracefully are so numerous, that there can be no escaping the conclusion that the people's right to freedom of expression and the leadership's obligation to be open to criticism was an indispensable part of the early Muslim political tradition. In fact, this remained so for quite some time even after the religiously inspired caliphal system of government which was primarily oriented to pleasing God changed, by stages, into a system in which the pursuit of worldly interests began to play an important role.

The third criterion for a sound political order is the prevalence of a general atmosphere of *shūrā* (consultation) as required by the Qur'ān (42:38). That the rulers should manage the collective affairs of Muslims by a process of mutual consultation is a religious imperative. Hence, to consult others in such matters has not been left to the discretion of the rulers. This is rather an established principle of Islamic collective life which has been emphaised by religious scholars throughout the fourteen centuries of Islamic history (see for instance, Ibn Taymiyyah) and continues to be emphasised by modern scholars (see for instnace, Muhammad 'Abduh).[10]

What it essentially signifies is that there is no basis in the *Sharī'ah* for despotism, dictatorship, and autocracy. The reason, as Shaykh Rashīd Riḍā has approvingly mentioned while reporting the opinion of Shaykh Muḥammad 'Abduh, is: "A group is generally farther from error than an individual, and the danger is much greater and for more serious for the *ummah* in entrusting its affairs to a single individual."[11] The *shūrā* that is required by Islam, however, is not of a cosmetic kind that would rubber-stamp the decisions of the rulers.

What is required is an autonomous institution for a free, unhindered and fearless discussion of all issues relating to public well-being within the framework of the *Sharī'ah*, and an earnest implementation by the executive of all the policies so formulated. The institution of *shūrā* demands widest possible participation of the people in the affairs of the state, either directly or through their representatives.[12] What specific form the implementation of this imperative may take is for the *ummah* to decide in the light of the circumstances obtaining at a given place and at a given time.

A fourth criterion for a sound political order is the the equality of all before law, and enforcement of incorruptible justice, as required by the Qur'ān: "And when you judge between people, judge with justice"(4:58). The rulings of the *Sharī'ah* should be applied equally to everyone, irrespective of status, wealth, or position of the person concerned in the social or governmental hierarchy.[13] Anything other than that is utter injustice and exploitation (*zulm*), and *zulm*, as Shaykh Muḥammad'Abduh has rightly emphasised, is the most hideous evil.[14] It is important to note here what Caliph Abū Bakr declared in his inaugural address: "The weak among you is strong in my sight until I have obtained for him his right, and the strong among you is weak in my sight until I have taken the right from him."[15] The message this conveys is that the *raison d'être* of the government is the establishment of justice and providing assistance to the weak and the poor to obtain their rights.

SATISFYING THE CRITERIA

The above-mentioned criteria for a sound political order can only be satisfied when those who wield political power derive their authority from the people and are answerable to them for the quality of their performance. In the present times this condition is best filled by free and fair elections. This also seems to be one of the implications of the Qur'ānic imperative to give the trust to those who deserve it(4:58). People must themselves give the trust willingly to those whom they consider to be deserving. It should not be acquired merely by dint of brute force or by way of patrimony.

It is significant that the leaders of the Islamic movements in the contemporary Muslim world (the founder of the Muslim Brotherhood for instance) have been strongly of the view that a democratic framework is in harmony with the genius of Islam. Ḥasan al-Bannā finds the representative form of government to be closest in spirit to Islamic political teachings.[16] Similarly, Mawlānā Mawdūdī emphasises that: "The government should be constituted and run in consultation with the people. Its structure must be such that the people are able to express their viewpoint. It is their will which should prevail. And this can take place only in a state that is democratic in structure and in its working."[17] Likewise, Shaykh 'Allāl al-Fāsī, President of Ḥizb al-Istiqlāl, has expressed similar views.[18] Accountability before the people in a democratic system is likely to ensure that the rulers of a Muslim country will abide by the *Sharī'ah* with respect to the well-being of all and the enforcement of justice.

This does not necessarily mean that the democratic form of government in its prevalent form is the ideal one and suffers from no no drawbacks. These drawbacks do not, however, justify the establishment of dictatorial or autocratic regimes. To the extent to which Muslims can reform the democratic process and remove, or even reduce, the influence of money, power and manipulation in the choice of political leadership, they will bring it closer to the Islamic ideal of *shūrā*. This will be an important step in the right direction. It might be difficult to accomplish the ideal in one stroke. It is likely to take place over a period of time and pass through a process of evolution.

ROLE OF THE *'ULAMĀ'*

While the role of the political leadership has, in general, left much to be desired, even the highly-placed and influential *'ulamā'* (religious scholars) and professionals, who carry considerable clout in the political set-up, have generally failed to play their role effectively. Instead of being the standard-bearers of socio-political reform and of putting their weight behind the moral and material uplift of the masses, quite a few of them have virtually acted as sycophants, often trying to secure for themselves as large a chunk of the national cake as possible.

They have often failed to recognise that Islamic values place a heavy responsibility on all those who occupy influential positions and require them to use their leverage fully in favour of socio-economic and political reform.[19] There is absolutely no justification for such people from the viewpoint of the *Sharī'ah* to serve their this-worldly self-interest by condoning, let alone collaborating with or becoming instruments of, the prevailing forces of corruption and injustice. Such behaviour has been equated by the Prophet, may the peace and blessings of God be on him, with disbelief.[20]

Within the existing unhealthy environment even those who are selfless and conscientious are unable to make significant headway, particularly when repressive governments feel threatened by reform and do their utmost to suppress and persecute the reformers. Hence the Prophet, may the peace and blessings of God be on him, had rightly predicted that:

> I am apprehensive of three things about my *ummah*: the lapse of the *'ulamā'*, the rule of the despots, and the pursuit of worldly pleasures.[21]

TWO FORMS OF CHANGE

The absence of socio-economic justice cannot, however, continue for long in the Muslim world. The masses are becoming increasingly restless and are craving for a change. Their restlessness is likely to find any one of two channels for expression. The most desirable of these channels would be to struggle for reform through peaceful and constitutional means. Such a struggle should aim at establishing a political order in which governments receive their mandate from the people. Once this has happened, the governments will be under constant pressure to strive for development with justice.

The resurgence of Islamic consciousness and sentiment will not allow the governments to continue to pay just lip service to Islam, as they have been wont do do. They will be under pressure to formulate and execute policies in the light of the Islamic strategy which, as we have already shown, would be the best way to achieve the well-being of the common people. If a sound political order is not established and reform movements are suppressed by use of brute force, popular restlessness might lead to the eruption of revolution. This would be unfortunate because it would not only entail a substantial loss of life and property, as has happened in many countries, but the ultimate outcome of such revolutions would also remain extremely uncertain.

Political reform, therefore, constitutes the cornerstone of all efforts at reform in the Muslim countries. This does not, however, mean that the establishment of a sound political order will automatically solve all problems. In our view a reformed political system will pave the way for other urgently needed socio-economic reforms, which will hopefully lead to a solution of the problems facing the people and a reduction in the prevailing inequities. The stronger the popular mandate, the more sincere and competent the leadership, and the greater the resources available in a Muslim country, the faster will be the tempo of socio-economic reforms and the improvement in the overall condition of the people.

> If the townsfolk had believed and acted righteously, We would indeed have opened out to them all kinds of blessings from the heaven and earth (Qur'ān, 7:96).

★★★

SIX

CONCLUSION

While even secular societies profess development with justice to be among their cherished goals, they continue to belittle the importance of having a clear sense of values and paying due attention to bringing about moral regeneration of the individuals and the society as important pillars in the scheme designed to achieve development in conjunction with justice. It is, nevertheless, generally acknowledged that development with justice requires a substantial and sustained increase in the allocation of resources for this purpose.

However, scarcity of resources does not permit such an increase, particularly because of the prevailing macroeconomic imbalances. Hence, what is needed is a reallocation of resources from uses that are inefficient and inequitable to uses that are efficient and equitable. How to bring about such a reallocation successfully remains an unanswered question.

The basic thesis of this book is that such a reallocation cannot be realised without the injection of a moral dimension into all individual and collective decisions that directly or indirectly affect the allocation and distribution of resources. In fact, it is not possible even to define efficiency and equity without the help of moral criteria. The secular orientation of the market system may enable it to reduce imbalances and foster higher growth, but it will not make it possible for it to bring about the kind of revolutionary changes that are needed in individual and collective behaviour for realising development with justice.

However, neo-classical economics continues to assert that the market system can help bring about such a reallocation in spite of its secular approach to the solution of human problems. It assumes that unhindered freedom to serve self-interest and to own and manage private property motivates the individuals to do their best. This maximises efficiency, which benefits not just the individual concerned but also the society.

All that needs to be done is to allow market forces to play their full role in the allocation and distribution of resources through market-determined prices (including interest rates and exchange rates). The policy prescription that emerges from this trend of thought is liberalisation of the economy to allow the market forces to play their legitimate role. There is no need for collective value judgements or for government intervention; the government should intervene only where the market fails to realise certain socially-desired goals. It should, however, do this as little as possible, and that too within the framework of Pareto optimality.

While liberalisation of the economy to let the individuals serve their self-interest does motivate them to render their best, it serves social interest only where social interest is in harmony with individual self-interest. For example, while higher prices may help reduce aggregate demand, they may not do this in an equitable manner if income and wealth are not equally distributed. Higher prices may not create any significant dent in the demand of the rich, who may continue to buy what they want in accordance with their individual preferences, many of which may not reflect social priorities.

In a secular society, there is nothing to motivate them to do otherwise. Resources thus get diverted to the production of what is needed by those who can cast more votes in the market place as a result of their own great wealth and the credit (that they are able to have access to on the basis of this wealth). Hence the poor get more squeezed. This frustrates the realisation of development with justice, and also leads to social unrest and political instability.

There is no doubt that some of the Far Eastern countries have been able to realise development with justice. This is, however, not due merely to liberalisation, even though liberalisation has acted as a catalyst. A configuration of other forces have played an important role. Some of these were: complementary role played by the governments in the economy to help rather than hinder the private sector, socio-economic equality generated by the drastic land reforms introduced by the occupying authorities, high propensity to save and invest resulting from this socio-economic equality and the cultural values of these societies, and high level of employment and self-employment facilitated by the labour-intensive techniques adopted by these countries. However, in spite of their initial development with justice, these countries are finding it difficult to perpetuate their socio-economic equality because of their adoption of the capitalist economic and financial institutions.

The two questions that, therefore, arise are: firstly, how to promote development with justice in countries where unusual war-related circumstances have not created socio-economic equality and where the values of hard and conscientious work and of simple living have not yet become internalised; and secondly, how to perpetuate and enhance the socio-economic equality once it has been realised?

Liberalisation alone will not be able to do this job, as we have shown in this book. A number of other measures need to be adopted. Firstly, the filtering effect of market-determined prices needs to be complemented by the moral filter to enable individuals and groups to evaluate their behaviour and their claims on resources from the point of view of their impact on social well-being. Secondly, individuals and groups need to be motivated appropriately to keep not just their self-interest but also the collective social interest in mind while expressing their preferences in the market place. Thirdly, the economy and financial intermediation need to be restructured in a way that would be conducive to the use of all available resources by the private as well as the public sectors for the realisation of development with justice. The government cannot, in this framework, behave as a passive onlooker. It must play a complementary role to guide and facilitate the efficient and equitable use of resources by the private sector.

The Islamic strategy is capable of doing this. While Islam has recognised the contribution that the basic tools of the market strategy (profit motive, private property, competition and decentralised decision-making) can make to efficiency, it has tried to ensure that human beings, who are the ends as well as the primary means of development and who are the ones who use the tools of the market strategy, are also reformed sufficiently to enable them to use these tools in a way that would serve their self-interest within the constraints of social well-being. It is just like supplying the guns to soldiers in the army. No one is free to use the gun as he pleases. Everyone is subject to certain rules even though the overall discipline of the army may itself be capable of ensuring the proper use of the gun. Likewise, while competition does serve as a constraint on self-interest, it may be restrained in a clandestine manner by unscrupulous entrepreneurs in the pursuit of their self-interest, unless there is an inner urge on their part not to act in a way that hurts the social interest.

Moral reform of the individual, along with his sense of accountability before the Supreme Being, Who can see everything, can help. Islam, however, does not confine itself merely to moral reform. It also introduces other important ingredients in its economic, financial and political systems to ensure that the scarce resources are used in accordance with the requirements of socio-economic justice.

Islamisation, which implies restructuring of the economy and changing the behaviour of individuals, institutions and the government in conformity with the Islamic strategy, can thus help humanise the market forces and enable them to contribute positively to goal realisation by improving and strengthening their role in the economy.

Hence, given the prevailing imbalances, inequities and political tensions in Muslim countries and the inability of both the market system and socialism to promote development with justice, the only feasible alternative they are left with is to Islamise their economies. Islamisation will not only help reduce the prevailing imbalances, but also make a perceptible contribution towards social harmony through the actualization of the *maqāṣid*. Self-interest, private property and market-determined prices will all have an important role to play. These will, however, be tempered by the humanising influence of other factors.

Of these, the concept of accountability before God will extend self-interest beyond the confines of this finite world and serve as a strong motivating force in keeping self-interest within the limits of social well-being. This, along with the filter of moral values, will help eliminate a substantial part of total claims on resources in an equitable manner by changing consumer preferences and government spending priorities before they even get expressed in the market place. The price filter could then take over, and the two together could help release resources for general need-fulfilment and also higher savings, investment and exports. Complementing this by a need-based production system and equitable material rewards should help create a favourable climate for greater efficiency, increased supply of need-satisfying goods and services, and lower prices for needs.

Land reforms and the proliferation of SMEs along with a total restructuring of the conventional financial system in the light of Islamic teachings should also make a positive contribution by lowering the concentration of wealth and power, expanding self-employment opportunities, and reducing poverty. Need-fulfilment and equitable distribution brought about in this manner should tend to have the effect of invigorating the human factor in development and of harnessing its energies and creativity for accelerated development. The reduction in inflationary pressures and the containment of the continuing depreciation in exchange rates should also make a positive contribution to growth and well-being.

Nevertheless, the interest of the poor should be attended to even further, not through a general subsidy, but rather through organised and intensified relief payments by the government and social organisations, out of *zakāh*, voluntary donations, and maximum possible budgetary appropriations.

The Muslim governments have unfortunately used Islam so far only as a slogan, failing to realise the positive contribution it can make towards the betterment of their societies and economies and to their own survival. Khurshid Ahmad has rightly indicated that "there is no evidence to conclude that, generally speaking, the policy makers derived any inspiration worth the name from Islam and tried to translate its economic ideals into development policies."[1]

Even with a change in attitudes and policies, the task of adjustment and reconstruction is bound to be difficult and time-consuming. The sooner the policy makers read the signs of the times, the better it will be for them and the *ummah*. Islamisation should not, however, be conceived as an panacea for all the problems of Muslim countries. Some of the problems created by centuries of social and moral degeneration, despotic rule, misguided domestic policies, and international economic, financial and exchange rate instability are bound to persist for a long time.

SUGGESTIONS FOR FURTHER READING

With regard to Chapters 2 and 3, the student may find it profitable to read anyone of the standard textbooks on development economics and to supplement it further, in keeping with his or her specific interest, by some of the books and papers indicated in the references and footnotes. It is, therefore, not necessary to add to them or to repeat them here. However, with respect to chapters 4-6 dealing with economic development within the Islamic perspective, the citations given in the footnotes and references may not be sufficient. The student may wish to read more to increase his or her grasp of the subject or to write papers on various issues raised in these chapters. To help in this task, a bibliography is being provided below which, though not comprehensive, would hopefully be of significant help. Since the subject is still nascent, there is a continuous flow of litterature and the interested reader may be able to keep abreast of the latest development with the help of the *Muslim World Book Review* and the *Index of Islamic Literature* published quarterly by the Islamic Foundation, Leicester, and the *International Institute of Islamic Thought*, Herndon, VA, USA.

NOTES AND REFERENCES

ONE: THE KIND OF DEVELOPMENT

[1]The fulfilment of basic needs is now quite widely accepted as a strategy for development (see Paul Streeten, "A Basic Needs Approach to Economic Development", in Kenneth P. Jameson and Charles K. Wilber, eds., *Directions in Economic Development*, Notre Dame: W. Notre Dame University Press, 1973; and Francis Stewart, *Basic Needs in Developing Countries*, Baltimore, Maryland: The John Hopkins University Press, 1955). A number of other authors have also written, over the last decade, on the concept of basic needs and its implications for development.

The stress on need-fulfilment in Islam should, however, not be construed as an afterthought arising out of the recent Western discussion of the subject. It has received an important place in the *Fiqh* and other Islamic literature throughout Muslim history. The jurists have unanimously held the view that it is the collective duty (*fard kifāyah*) of the Muslim society to take care of the basic needs of the poor (see, for example, Abū Muḥammad ʿAlī Ibn Ḥazm, *al-Muḥallā*, Beirut: al-Maktab al-Tijārī, n.d., vol. 6, p. 156:725). In fact, according to Shāṭibī, this is the *raison d'étre* of the society itself (Abū Isḥāq al-Shāṭibī, *al-Muwāfaqāt fī Uṣūl al-Sharīʿah*, ed., ʿAbd Allāh Darāz, Cairo: al-Maktabah al-Tijāriyyah al-Kubrā, n.d., vol. 2, p. 177). All modern writers, including Mawdūdī, Sayyid Qutb, Musṭafā al-Sibāʿī, Abū Zahrah, Muḥammad Bāqir al-Ṣadr, Muḥammad al-Mubārak, and Yūsuf al-Qaraḍāwī, are unanimously agreed on this point (see, for a brief introduction, M. N. Siddiqi, "Guarantee of a Minimum Level of Living in Islamic State", in Munawar Iqbal, *Distributive Justice and Need Fulfilment in an Islamic Economy* (Islamabad: International Institute of Islamic Economics, 1986), pp.249–301; ʿAbd al-Salām al-ʿAbbādī, *al-Milkiyyah fī al-Sharīʿah al-Islāmiyyah* (Cairo: al-Maṭbaʿah al-Salafiyyah, 1349 A.H.); and M. Anas Zarqa, "Islamic Distributive Schemes", in Munawar Iqbal, *Distributive Justice and Need Fulfilment, op. cit.*, pp. 163–219.

[2]From ʿUbādah ibn al-Ṣāmit and Ibn ʿAbbās in Ibn Mājah, *Sunan*, Abwāb al-Aḥkām, Bāb man banā fī haqqihi mā yaḍurru bi jārihi; also reported by Aḥmad and Dār Quṭnī. This *ḥadīth* is considered by al-Qurashī to be one of the five fundamental *aḥādīth* on which the derivative principles of *Fiqh* are based (see, Yaḥyā ibn Ādam al-Qurashī, *Kitāb al-Kharāj*, ed., Aḥmad Muḥammad Shākir, Cairo: al-Maṭbaʿah al-Salafiyyah, 1384 A.H., p.93). The *ḥadīth* has become Article 13 of the 100 maxims of Islamic jurisprudence embodied in the Ḥanafī *Fiqh* compendium called the *Majallah*.

[3]See M. Anas Zarqa, "Capital Allocation, Efficiency and Growth in an Interest-free Islamic Economy", *Journal of Economics and Administrative Sciences* (Jeddah), November 1982, p.49; and "Islamic Economics: An Approach to Human Welfare", in K. Ahmad, *Studies in Islamic Economics* (Leicester, U.K.: The Islamic Foundation, 1980), pp. 3—18. See also Benjamin Ward, *What's Wrong with Economics* (London: Macmillan, 1972). p. 211.

[4]Frank H. Knight, "Social Economic Organization", reprinted from his *The Economic Organization*, pp. 3—30, in W. Breit, *et. al.*, *Readings in Microeconomics* (St. Louis: Times Mirror/Mosley, 1986), p.4. I am grateful to Dr. Anas Zarqa who drew my attention to this argument.

TWO: CAN SECULARISM FOSTER JUST DEVELOPMENT?

[1]Bertrand Russel, *A History of Western Philosophy* (New York: Simon and Schuster, 1945), p. 775.

[2]There is no doubt that few economists would now be willing to support this view. It is, however, a logical outcome of the assumed symmetry between public and private interests and was widely held by economists like J. B. Clark who felt that factor incomes in the real world closely approximated the marginal product and its value. See G. Stigler, *Production and Distribution Theories: The Formative Period* (New York: Macmillan, 1941). It, therefore, provided the rationale for the much-cherished governmental non-intervention principle.

[3]Paul Samuelson, *Economics* (New York: McGraw Hill, 1980, 11th ed.), p.591.

[4]Arthur Okun, *Equality and Efficiency: the Big Trade-off* (Washington, D.C.: Brookings Institution, 1975), p.11.

[5]R. H. Tawney, *The Acquisitive Society* (New York: Harcourt and Brace, 1948), p.12.

[6]I. Adelman and C.T. Morris, *Economic Growth and Social Equity in Developing Countries* (Standord, California: Standord Union Press, 1973), p.189.

[7]See Richard Titmus, *Commitment to Welfare* (London: George Allen and Unwin, 2nd ed., 1976), p.196.

THREE: THE INCONSISTENCY OF DEVELOPMENT ECONOMICS

[1]See, Walt W. Rostow, *Theorists of Economic Growth from David Hume to the Present: with a Perspective on the Next Century* (New York: Oxford

University Press, 1990), and the review article on this book by Robert Dorfman, in the *Journal of Economic Literature*, June 1991, pp. 573–91.

[2]Arndt, H.W., *Economic Development: The History of an Idea* (Chicago: University of Chicago Press, 1987).

[3]Eugene Staley, *The Future of Underdeveloped Countries* (New York, 1954), pp. 4, 21 and 24; see also Bert F. Hoselitz, *Sociological Aspects of Economic Growth* (New York: The Free Press, 1960), p. 56. Staley has been described by Arndt as "the man who more than any other brought the theme of economic development into the American discussion". (See H.W. Arndt, "Development Economics before 1945," in Bhagwati and Eckaus, *Development and Planning: Essays in Honour of Paul Rosentein-Rodan* (Cambridge, Mass.: The MIT Press, 1972), p.26.

[4]Gunnar Myrdal, *Asian Drama* (New York: The Twentieth Century Fund, 1968), vol. 2, p. 73. According to Streeten, Myrdal's *Asian Drama*, is on the whole, pessimistic about the development prospects of developing countries. See Paul Streeten, *Development Perspective* (London: Macmillan, 1981), p.425. Myrdal's "modernisation ideals" were: rationality, social and economic equalisation, efficiency, diligence, orderliness, punctuality, frugality, scruplulous honesty, rationality in decisions on action, preparedness for change, alertness to opportunities, energetic enterprise, integrity and self-reliance, cooperativeness and willingness to take the long view" (*ibid.*, vol.1, pp. 57–69). It is surprising how Myrdal could believe that all these ideals are "indigenous" to the West and "alien" to all developing (including Muslim) countries.

[5]See, United Nations, *Measures for the Econoic Development of Underdeveloped Countries* (New York: United Nations, 1951), pp. 13–16; C.P. Kindleberger, "Review of The Economy of Turkey; The Economic Development of Guatemala; Report on Cuba, *Review of Economics and Statistics*, November 1952, pp. 391–2; and Joseph P. Spengler, "IBRD Mission, Growth Theory", *American Economic Review*, May 1954, pp.586–7.

[6]Ragnar Nurkse, *Problems of Capital Formation in Underdeveloped Countries* (Oxford:Basil, Blackwell, 1953), p.4.

[7]For examples of relatively pessimistic predictions for particular countries, see IBRD, *The Basis of a Programme for Columbia* (Washington, D.C.: IBRD, 1950); Willard Thorp, "Some Basic Policy Issues in Economic Development", *American Economic Review*, May 1951, pp. 407–17; G. E. Britnell, "Factors in the Economic Development of Ceylon", *American Economic Review*, May 1953, pp. 115–25. See also W. A. Lewis, "A Review of Economic Development", *Manchester School*, May 1965, pp.1–16.

[8]H. F. Williamson in his comments on Moses Abramovitz, "Economics of Growth", in B.F. Haley, *A Survey of Contemporary Economics* (Homewood, Ill.: Irwin, 1952), vol. 2, p.182.

[9]Arthur W. Lewis, "Reflections on Development," in Gustav Ranis and T. Paul Schultz, *The State of Development Economics: Progress and Perspectives* (Oxford: Blackwell, 1988), pp.3—14 and 16—19.

[10]Harvey Leibenstein, *Economic Backwardness and Economic Growth* (New York: John Wiley, 1957), pp.96 and 98.

[11]Some of the economists whose writings were instrumental in providing various elements of the socialist strategy were: Nurkse, Myrdal, Hirschman, Balogh, Rosenstein Rodan, Chenery, Prebisch, Singer, and Streeten. Those who continued to emphasise the superiority of the market were: Haberler, Viner, Bauer and Yamey, and Schultz. For detailed references, see Deepak Lal, *The Poverty of Development Economics* (London: Hobart Paperback No.16, 1984), p.5.

[12]See for example, Albert Hirschman, "The Rise and Decline of Development Economics", in *Essays in Trespassing* (New York: Cambridge University Press, 1981); and Gunnar Myrdal, *Economic Theory and Underdeveloped Regions* (London: Buckworth, 1957).

[13]See W. W. Rostow, "Take-off into Self-Sustained Economic Growth", *Economic Journal*, March 1986.

[14]Myrdal, *Asian Drama, op. cit.,* vol. 3, pp. 1899 and 1900.

[15]Gottfried Haberler, "Liberal and Illiberal Development Policy", in Gerald M. Meier, (ed.), *Pioneers in Development* (New York: Oxford University Press, 1987) p. 66.

[16]The literature on economic development is full of assertions that an improvement in income distribution is in direct conflict with economic growth. For a summary of these views, see Willam R. Cline, *Potential Effects of Income Redistribution on Economic Growth* (New York: Praeger, 1973), chapter 2.

[17]Arthur W. Lewis, *The Theory of Economic Growth* (Homewood, Ill.: Richard D. Irwin, 1955), p.9.

[18]Peter T. Bauer and Basil S. Yamey, *The Economics of Underdeveloped Countries* (Chicago: The University of Chicago Press, 1957), p.168.

[19]United Nations, ECAFE, "Crieria for Allocating Investment Resources among Various Fields of Development in Underdeveloped Countries", June 1961, P.30.

[20]Harry G. Johnson, *Money, Trade and Economic Growth* (London: George Allen and Unwin, 1962), p.159.

[21]Irma Adelman and Erik Thorbecke (eds.), *Theory and Design of Economic Development* (Baltimore: Johns Hopkins, 1966); see also, G. Fields, "Income Distribution and Economic Growth", in Ranis and Schultz, *Sate of Development Economics, op. cit.,* p.460.

[22]P.T. Bauer and B.S. Yamey, *The Economics of Underdeveloped Countries* (Chicago: The University of Chicago Press, 1957), p.168. See also W. Galenson and H. Leibenstein, "Investment Criteria, Productivity and Economic Development", *Quarterly Journal of Economics*, August (1955), pp.343–70.

[23]Simon Kuznets, "Economic Growth and Income Inequality", *American Economic Review*, March 1955; "Quantitative Aspects of the Economic Growth of Nations: VIII, Distribution of Income by Size", *Economic Development and Cultural Change*, January (1963); and *Modern Economic Growth* (New Haven: Yale University Press, 1966).

[24]See J. G. Williamson and P. H. Lindert, *American Inequality: A Macro-Economic History* (New York: Academic Press, 1980); J. G. Williamson, *Did British Capitalism Breed Inequality?* (London: Allen and Unwin, 1985); and J. G. Williamson, "The Historical Content of the Classical Labour Surplus Model",*Population and Development Review*, June (1985), pp.171–91. See also Williamson's comments on Lewis' paper in Ranis and Schultz, *State o, Development Economics, op. cit.,* p.29.

[25]Bauer and Yamey, *op. cit.,* p.206. See also p.168.

[26]Lewis, *Theory of Economic Growth, op. cit.,* pp.404–406.

[27]"Strategy of the Third Plan", *Problems in the Third Plan — A Critical Miscellany*, p.50.

[28]Mahboobul Haq, *The Strategy of Economic Planning: A Case Study of Pakistan* (Karachi: Oxford University Press, 1963), p.30.

[29]Myrdal, *Asian Drama, op. cit.,* vol. 2, p.740.

[30]*Ibid.,* p. 808.

[31]*Ibid.,* p. 807.

[32]David Morawetz, *Twenty-Five Years of Economic Development: 1950—1975* (Washington, D.C.: IBRD, 1977), p.9.

[33]This may be clearly seen from the identity, $Y=C+I+G+X-M$, where Y=gross domestic product; C=consumption; I=gross domestic investment; G=government spending; X=exports; and M=imports. If $C+I+G=A$, where A represents gross domestic absorption, then $Y=(A-M)+X$. For developing countries, which are encountering both internal and external imbalances, a successful strategy to raise Y and lower the imbalances would require a rise not only in X but also in $(A-M)$, which is the domestic absorpiton of domestically-produced goods and services. Since A needs to be reduced to remove the internal imbalance, the only way $(A-M)$ may be raised is by lowering M more than in proportion to the decline in A. Although import-substitution can be an important way to realise this goal, it would not be sufficient. It would also be necessary to substantially squeeze the import of luxury and inessential consumer goods so that the import of essential consumer and capital goods proceeds as desired.

[34]Douglas Dosser, "General Investment Criteria for Less Developed Countries", *Scottish Journal of Political Economy*, June (1962), pp.93—8.

[35]Hla Myint, "Neoclassical Development Analysis: its Strengths and Limitations", in Gerald M. Meier, *Pioneers in Development*, second edition, (New York: Oxford University Press, 1987), *op. cit.*, p.118.

[36]UNCTAD's *Trade and Development Report 1989* pours some cold water on the idea that trade policy reforms necessarily promote the economic growth of developing countries. A study of thirty-two developing countries which followed varying trade policies during the 1980s, revealed that favourable export performance was not always synonymous with good overall economic performance. See also, "Export Reforms No Guarantee of Economic Growth", *Financial Times*, 6 September 1989, p.6.

[37]Peter Winglee, "Agricultural Trade Policies of Industrial Countries", *Finance and Development*, March 1989, p.10.

[38]See, Sam Laird and Alexander Yeats, "Non-Tariff Barriers of Developed Countries, 1966—68", *Finance and Development*, March (1989), pp.12—13.

[39]United Nations Conference on Trade and Development (CTAD), *Trade and Development Report 1985*, pp.123—4. For the external debt of developing countries, see note 65.

[40]See Hollis Chenery with A. Strout, "Foreign Assistance and Economic Development", *American Economic Review*, September 1966; and Henry Bruton, "The Two-Gap Approach to Aid and Development", *American Economic Review*, September (1966).

[41]The average anual rate of inflation has continually risen in developing countries from 10 percent per annum in 1965—73 to 26 percent in 1974—82, 51 percent in 1983-87, and 81.4 percent in 1988—90 (IBRD, *World Development Report 1989,* p.62; and IMF, *International Financial Statistics,* November 1991, p.69).

[42]Haberler, in Meier, *Pioneers in Development, op. cit.,* p.70.

[43]Henry Bruton, *Inflation in a Growing Economy* (Bombay: University of Bombay, 1961), p.57.

[44]Ibid., p.58.

[45]Lewis, in Ranis and Schultz, *State of Development Economics, op. cit.,* p.22.

[46]The total external debt of all developing countries rose from $639 billion in 1980 to a projected $1,341 billion in 1990   (IBRD, *World Debt Tables: External Debt of Developing Countries 1990—91,* vol. 1, p.12).

[47]Gerald Meier, *Leading Issues in Development Economics: Selected Materials and Commentary* (New York: Oxford University Press, 1964), p.563.

[48]J. K. Galbraith, *Economic Development in Perspective* (Cambridge, Mass.: Harvard University Press, 1962), pp.9—10.

[49]Michael Camdessus, "Opening Remarks", Vittori Corbo, *et. al., Growth-Oriented Adjustment Programmes* (Washington, D.C.: IMF/IBRD, 1987), p.7.

[50]Morawetz, *Twenty-Five Years, op. cit.,* p.10.

[51]*Ibid.,* p.71.

[52]Gerald Meier, *Emerging from Poverty: The Economics that Really Matters* (New York: Oxford University Press, 1984), pp.5 and 184.

[53]Cited by Meier, *Emerging from Poverty, op. cit.,* p.29.

[54]Cited by Meier, *Emerging from Poverty, op. cit.,* p.2.

[55]Meier, *Emerging from Poverty, op. cit.,* p.2.

[56]Dudley Seers "The Meaning of Development", *International Development Review,* December (1969).

[57]Barber Conable, "Opening Remarks", Corbo, *et. al., Growth-Oriented Adjustment Programme, op. cit.,* p.6.

[58]IMF, *Fund-Supported Programmes, Fiscal Policy, and Income Distribution,* IMF Occasional Paper No. 46 (September 1986), p.1.

[59]IMF, *The Implication of Fund-Supported Adjustment Programmes for Poverty: Experience of Selected Countries*, Occasional Paper No. 58(1988), pp. 1 and 32. See also *Theoretical Aspects of the Design of Fund-Supported Adjustment Programmes*, Occasional Paper No. 55, September 1987.

[60]IMF, *Implication of Fund Supported Adjustment*. Occasional Paper No. 58 (1988), p.17.

[61]See Ronald Findlay, "Trade, Development and the State", in Ranis and Schultz, *State of Development Economics, op. cit.*, pp.92—3; see also Myint in Meier, *Pioneers in Development, op. cit.*, p.117.

[62]See Ronald Findley's comments on Haberler, in Meier, *Pioneers in Development, op. cit.*, p.96; see also Bhagwati and Kruger, "Exchange Control, Liberalisation and Development", *American Economic Review*, 2(1973), pp.419—27.

[63]Yasuo Masai, "Japan", *The New Encyclopaedia Britannica*, 15th ed., vol. 10, p.49.

[64]Marius B. Jansen, "Japan, History of", *The New Encyclopaedia Britannica*, 15th ed., vol. 10. p.88; *Agriculture in Korea* (Seoul: Ministry of Agriculture and Forestry, 1970), pp.5—17; and Oh Young-Kyun, "Agrarian Reform and Economic Development: A Case Study of Korean Agriculture", *Koreana Quarterly* (1969), p.99.

[65]Australian Bureau of Agricultural and Research Economics, *Japanese Agricultural Policies*, Policy Monograph No. 3, Canberra, (1988).

[66]Jeffery D. Sachs, "Trade and Exchange Rate Policies in Growth-Oriented Adjustment", in Corbo, *et. al.*, *Growth Oriented Adjustment Programmes, op. cit.*, p.301.

[67]*Ibid.*, p.303.

[68]Jeffrey Sachs, *Social Conflict and Populist Policies in Latin America* (Cambridge, Mass.: National Burea of Economic Research, Paper No.2897).

[69]Pranab Bardhan's comments on Ranis and Fei, in Ranis and Schultz, *State of Development Economics, op. cit.*, p.138.

[70]Meier, *Emerging from Poverty, op.cit.*, p.61.

[71]See Hla Myint, "Comparative Analysis of Taiwan's Economic Development with Other Countries", *Academic Economic Papers*, March 1982; see also Myint, in Meier, *Pioneers in Development, op. cit.*, p.133.

[72]Ranis and Fei, in Ranis and Schultz, *State of Development Economics*, *op. cit.*, p.121.

[73]See, Meier, *Emerging from Poverty*, *op. cit.*, p.63; Tibor Scitovosky, "Economic Development in Taiwan and South Korea", Food Research Institute Studies, No. 4 (1985), pp.215—64; and "Unequalled Economic Failures", *The Economist*, 17 June 1989, p.83. According to Meier, Taiwan "is probably the most egalitarian of all capitalist countries" (Meier, *Emerging from Poverty*, *op. cit.*, p.63). This statement is probably inaccurate because a number of other countries have a lower Gini coefficient and better welfare services than those of Taiwan.

[74]With respect to Japan, see R. Benedict, *The Chrysanthemum and the Sword* (Boston: Houghton Mifflin, 1946); see also Yoshihara Kunion, *Japanese Economic Development: A Short Introduction* (Tokyo: Oxford University Press, 1979), pp.80—82.

[75]For Japan, see T. Nakamura, (tr.) J. Kaminski, *The Pos-twar Japanese Economy: Its Development and Structure* (Tokyo: University of Tokyo Press, 1981), p.96.

[76]World Bank, *World Tables, 1988—89*, vol. 1, pp. 66—9; and Directorate General of Budget, Accounting and Statistics, Republic of Taiwan, *Statistical Yearbook of the Republic of China, 1988*, p. 90.

[77]In 1983, Japan's average tariff rate was 4.5 percent for dutiable imports and 2.5 percent for all imports, lower than in America or Europe. Even in textitles the tariff of 13.8 percent was lower than America's 22.7 percent and about the same as in Europe. "An Open and Shut Case", in "Japan: A Survey", *The Economist*, 7 October 1985, p.20.

[78]Lester Thurow, "A Time to Dismantle the World Economy", *The Economist*, 9 November 1985, p.23.

[79]Findlay, in Ranis and Schultz, *State of Development Economics*, *op. cit.*, p.90.

[80]See IMF, *Government Financial Statistics Yearbook 1989*, pp. 92—3, for data on worldwide defence spending, except Japan for which data have been obtained from other sources.

[81]OECD, *Revenue Statistics of OECD Member Countries, 1965—89* (1990).

[82]"Republic of Korea [Sourth Korea]", *The Europa Yearbook 1987*, pp.1661—62.

[83]See Parvez Hasan, *Korea: Problems and Issues in a Rapidly Growing Economy* (Baltimore: The Johns Hopkins University Press, published for the World Bank, 1976), p.23.

[84]Data for 1965 from Michael Prowse, "Unequal Society Rethinking its Priorities", *The Financial Times*, 15 June 1989, p. XII; and those for 1987 from the IBRD, *World Development Report 1989*, p.223.

[85]Liz McGregor, "Labour Unrest, the Price of Success", *The International Herald Tribune*, 5 July 1989, p.7.

[86]Prowse, *Unequal Society Rethinking its Priorities, op. cit.*

[87]Hasan, *Korea, op. cit.*, p.23.

[88]Kunion, *Japanese Economic Development, op. cit.*, p.111.

[89]The ten largest Japanese banks, many of them associated with the names of Zaibatsu families, are Dai-Ichi Kangyo, Mitsui Taiyo Kobe, Sumitome, Fuji, Mitsubishi, Sanwa, Tokai, Daiwa, Bank of Tokyo, and Kyowa. Some of these banks are among the largest in the world, (see "Wedding Bells for Japan's Big Banks", *The Economist*, 2 September 1989, p.79; and "Ranking the World's Largest Banks", *Institutional Investor*, June (1989), pp.119 ff.).

[90]Forty-eight percent of all wholesale stores and eighty-five percent of all retail stores were classified as small-scale in 1985 (i.e., they had less than five employees). These, however, accounted for only five percent of the value of all wholesale and thirty-one percent of retail sales in that year (Japan: Ministry of International Trade and Industry, *Commercial Statistics and White Paper on International Trade 1988*).

[91]This is clearly reflected in the Gini coefficient for Japan, which rose from 0.380 in 1965 to 0.420 in 1971 (see Tibor Scitovosky, "Economic Development in Taiwan and South Korea", *Food Research Institute Studies*, 4(1985), pp.215–64.

[92]*Forbes Magazine*, cited by *Arab News*, 10 July 1989, p.14.

[93]See Karel van Wolferen, *The Enigma of Japanese Power* (London: Macmillan, 1989).

[94]Yamaichi Research Institute of Securities and Economics, *Monthly Digest of Statistics*, January and September 1989 and July 1990, p. 1.

[95]*Ibid.*, pp. 6 and 126.

[96]Nikko Research Centre, *Analysis of Japanese Industries for Investors, 1990* (January, 1990), p.202.

[97]According to Bill Emmott: "By leading a fancier and more visibly opulent life, the new rich are setting an example to the millions who have only moderate wealth. The effect of their riches is trickling down, affecting what people spend, why they buy and what they aspire to. The old, austere homogeneity of Japanese life is breaking down." (Bill Emmott, *The Sun also Sets: Why Japan will not be Number One* (Hampstead, U.K.: Simon and Schuster, 1989).

[98]See "South Korea: Land to the Dweller", *The Economist*, 16 September 1989, p. 80; and "A Dangerous Game in Taipei: Taiwan's Stock Market was once a Sleepy Casino, Now it's Hyperactive", *Ibid.*, 9 September 1989, p.113. See also the special surveys on Taiwan and South Korea, *Financial Times*, 10 October 1989 and 16 May 1990.

[99]Meier, "On Getting Policies Right", in Meier, *Pioneers in Development*, *op. cit.*, p.70.

[100]Morawetz, *Twenty-Five Years*, *op. cit.*, p.71.

[101]Gary Fields, "Income Distribution and Economic Growth", in Ranis and Schultz, *State of Development Economics*, *op. cit.*, pp.468—9.

[102]Morawetz, *Twenty-Five Years*, *op. cit.*, p.7.

[103]See Deepak Lal, *The Poverty of Development Economics*, *op.cit.*

[104]Meier, *Emerging from Poverty*, *op.cit.*, p.233.

[105]*Ibid.*, p.228.

[106]*Ibid.*, p.90.

[107]Development Committee, *Strengthening Efforts to Reduce Poverty* (Washington, D.C.: World Bank, 1989).

[108]*Ibid.*, p.5.

FOUR: THE ISLAMIC STRATEGY

[1]For discussion, see M. U. Chapra, *Objectives of the Islamic Economic Order* (Leicester, U.K. The Islamic Foundation, 1979), pp. 14—16. See also Hakim Mohammad Said (ed.), *The Employer and the Employee: Islamic Concept* (Karachi: Hamdard Academy, 1972).

[2]See M. U. Chapra, *Towards a Just Monetary System* (Leicester, U.K.: The Islamic Foundation, 1985), pp. 107—25. See also Mohsin S. Khan and Abbas Mirakhor, *Theoretical Studies in Islamic Banking and Finance* (Houston,

Texas: The Institute for Research and Islamic Studies, 1987); Muhammad Ariff, *Monetary and Fiscal Economics of Islam* (Jiddah: International Centre for Research in Islamic Economics, 1982); M. Nejatullah Siddiqi, "Rationale of Islamic Banking", in *Issues in Islamic Banking* (Leicester, U.K.: The Islamic Foundation, 1983), pp. 67—96; and Ziauddin Ahmad, *Concepts and Models of Islamic Banking* (Karachi: Institute of Bankers in Pakistan, 1984).

[3]For a more detailed discussion of the moral characteristics required of a true Muslim see, Sayyid Abu'l A'lā Mawdūdī, *The Islamic Movement: the Dynamics of Values, Power and Change* (1984), in particular pp.93—192. See also Marwan Ibrahim al-Kaysi, *Morals and Manners in Islam: a Guide to Islamic Ādāb* (Leicester, U.K.: The Islamic Foundation, 1986), see particularly the Introduction, pp.13—53.

[4]See 'Abd al-Salām al-'Abbādī, *al-Milkiyyah fī al-Sharī'ah al-Islāmiyyah* (Amman, Jordan: Maktabah al-Aqṣā, 1974—1975), vol. 2, p.400.

[5]See Ḥasan al-Bannā, *Majmū'at Rasā'il al-Imām al-Shahīd Ḥasan al-Bannā* (Alexandria: Dār al-Da'wah, 1989), p.266; Sayyid Abū al-A'lā Mawdūdī, who, in his earlier writings, held the opinion that no 'arbitrary' limits may be imposed on land ownership, modified his stand later and stated that, in the light of the existing unfair distribution of land, the Islamic state may, and even should, impose certain desired limits as a temporary measure to remove inequities (see Mawdūdī, *Mas'alah Milkiyyat-i Zamīn* (Lahore: Islamic Publications, 3rd ed., 1969), p.111. See also Muḥammad Quṭb, *al-Insān Bayn al-Māddiyyah wa al-Islām* (Cairo: 'Īsā al-Bābī al-Ḥalabī, 4th ed., 1965), pp.160—68 and 200—1; Muṣṭafā al-Sibā'ī, *Ishtirākiyyat al-Islām* (Damascus: Mu'assassat al-Maṭbū'āt al-'Arabiyyah, 2nd ed., 1960), p.62; al-'Abbādī, *al-Milkiyyah, op.cit.*, vol.2, pp.398—520; and Rafīq al-Miṣrī, *Uṣūl al-Iqtiṣād al-Islāmi* (Damascus: Dār al-Qalam, 1989), pp.53—4. There are many others who have expressed similar opinions, for example, 'Alī al-Khafīf, Maḥmūd Abū Sa'ūd, Muḥammad Yūsuf Mūsā, Wahbah al-Zuhaylī, 'Abd al-Ḥāmid Mitwallī, Muḥammad Anīs Ibrāhīm.

[6]For a very cogent summary, see Yūsuf al-Qaraḍāwī, *al-Ḥalāl wa al-Ḥarām fī al-Islām* (Cairo: Dār al-I'tiṣām, 8th ed., 1974), pp.290—301; al-'Abbādī, *al-Milkiyyah, op. cit.*, vol. 2, pp.113—28; and M. Anas Zarqā, "al-Siyāsat al-Iqtiṣādiyyah wa al-Takhṭīṭ fī al-Iqtiṣād al-Islāmī", *al-Idārah al-Māliyyah fī al-Islām* (Amman: al-Majma' al-Malikī li Buhūth al-Ḥaḍārah al-Islāmiyyah, 1990), vol. 3, pp. 1259—63.

[7]This opinion is based on a number of *ahādīth*, one of which, reported by Jābir ibn 'Abd Allāh, says: "The Prophet, may the peace and blessings of God be on him, prohibited the taking of rent or share on land" (*Saḥīḥ Muslim*, Cairo: 'Īsā al-Bābī al-Ḥalabī, 1955, vol. 3, p.1186:90). Another *hadīth*, also reported by Jābir ibn 'Abd Allāh, says: "Whoever has land, let him cultivate

it himself; if he does not do so, let him have his brother do so" (*Ṣaḥīḥ Muslim*, p.1176:88). See also other *aḥādīth* of similar meaning in the sections on lease of land (*kirā' al-arḍ*), and grant of land (*al-arḍ tumnaḥ*) on pp.1176—80 and 1184—5). This point of view was held by a number of jurists like 'Aṭā', Makḥūl, Mujāhid, Ḥasan al-Baṣrī and, according to a report, also by Awzā'ī (see Ibn Ḥazm, *al-Muḥallā*, vol. 8, p.213). See also, 'Abd al-Ḥamīd Abū Sulaymān, "The Theory of the Economics of Islam", in *Contem-porary Aspects of Economic Thinking in Islam* (Bloomington, Indiana: MSA, 1976), pp.9—12.

[8]For a strong case in favour of this contention, see Ibn Ḥazm, *al-Muḥallā*, vol.8, pp.210—14; see also Qaraḍāwī, *al-Ḥalāl wa al-Ḥarām*, *op. cit.*, pp.295—99.

[9]For a strong case in its favour, see Abū Yūsuf, *Kitāb al-Kharāj* (Cairo: al-Maṭba'ah al-Salafiyyah, 2nd ed., 1353 A.H.), pp. 88—91; and Ibn Taymiyyah, *al-Ḥisbah fī al-Islām* (Damascus: Maktabah Dār al-Bayān, 1967), pp. 28—31; see also Mawdūdī, *Mas'alah, op.cit.*

[10]Al-'Abbādī, *al-Milkiyyah, op. cit.*, vol. 2, p. 127, and Ibn Taymiyyah, *al-Ḥisbah, op. cit.*, p.30.

[11]See the comments of Dr. Anas Zarqa on the paper of Ahmad Mustafa and Hossein Askari, "The Economic Implications of Land Ownership and Land Cultivation in Islam", in Munawar Iqbal (ed.), *Distributive Justice, op.cit.*, pp.152—3. The reference Dr. Zarqa cites for Mālik's view is al-Bājjī, *al-Muntaqā Sharḥ al-Muwaṭṭa*, vol. 5, pp. 146—8.

[12]Al-'Abbādī, *al-Milkiyyah, op. cit.*, vol.2, p. 128, and M. Anas Zarqa in M. Iqbal (ed.), *Distributive Justice, op. cit.*, p.153. For some of the legal reforms suggested by Mawlānā Mawdūdī to regulate the relationship between landlords and tenants, see *Islām aur Jadīd Ma'āshī Naẓariyyāt* (Urdu), (Lahore: Islamic Publications, 1959), pp.152—4.

[13]N. T. Quan and A. Y. C. Koo, "Concentration of Land Holdings: an Explanation of Kuznet's Conjecture", *Journal of Development Economics*, 18 (1985), pp.101—17.

[14]See C. Gonzales-Vega and V. H. Cespedes, *Growth and Equity: Changes in Income Distribution in Costa Rica* (New York: United Nations, 1983); K. Griffin and A. R. Khan, "Poverty in the Third World: Ugly Facts and Fancy Models", *World Development*, 6 (1978), pp.1271—80; ILO, *Poverty and Landless in Rural Asia* (Geneva: ILO, 1977); A. R. Khan and P. D. Weldon, "Income Distribution and Levels of Living in Java, 1963—70", *Economic Development and Cultural Change*, 25 (1985), pp.699—711; S. R. Osmani and A. Rahman, *Income Distribution in Bangladesh* (New York: United Nations, 1983); E. Lee, "Egalitarian Peasant Farming and Rural Development: the Case

of South Korea", *World Development*, 7 (1979), pp.493—519; D. G. Rao, "Economic Growth and Equity in the Republic of Korea", *World Development*, 6 (1978), pp. 397—409.

[15]See S. A. Berry and W. R. Cline, *Agrarian Structure and Productivity in Developing Countries* (Baltimore: Johns Hopkins University Press, 1979); Subrata Ghatak, "Agriculture and Economic Development", in Normam Gemmell, *Surveys in Development Economics* (Oxford: Basil Blackwell, 1987), pp. 355—6; and P.A. Yotopoulos and J. B. Nugent, *Economics of Development* (New York: Harper and Row, 1976), p.6.

[16]Ghatak, in Gemmell, *Surveys, op. cit.*, p.356.

[17]See IBRD, *World Development Report 1982*, pp.81 and 91.

[18]IBRD, *World Development Report 1982*, pp.85—109.

[19]IBRD, *Poverty and Hunger: Issues and Options for Food Security in Developing Countries, 1986*.

[20]U.S. House of Representatives, *Report, of the Select Committee of Higher Banking for the Poor: Alleviating Poverty through Credit Assistance to the Poorest Micro-Entrepreneurs in Developing Countries* (Washington D.C.: U.S. Government Printing Office, May 1986), p.1.

[21]In Japan three out of four farming households now get most of their income from outside agriculture. See "When the Salt of the Earth Loses its Savour", *Economist*, 20 February, 1988, pp.43—4.

[22]The alternative arrangement, in which cooperative societies, commercial banks, and government sponsored financial institutions will have to play an important role, must avoid interest and be based on risk/reward sharing (*mudārabah* or *mushārakah*), *murābahah* (cost-plus financing), leasing or *bay' salam*. *Bay' salam* refers to a sale where full payment is made in advance against an obligation to deliver the specified tangible goods at an agreed future date. This is not the same as a speculative forward sale because full, and not margin, payment is required. Under this arrangement, the farmer may be able to secure the needed financing by making an advance sale of only a part of his expected output. This will not get him into delivery problems in case of a fall in output due to unforeseen circumstances. For details on *bay' salam* see 'Abd al-Raḥmān al-Jazīrī, *Kitāb al-Fiqh 'alā al-Madhāhib al-Arba'ah* (Cairo: al-Maktabah al-Tijāriyyah al-Kubrā, 1938), vol. 3, pp.3—20 and vol. 2, pp.302—18.

[23]See Paul A. Baran and Paul M. Sweezy, *Monopoly Capital: An Essay on the American Economic and Social Order* (New York: Modern Reader Paperback, 1966), p.6.

[24]See C. Wright Mills, *The Power Elite* (New York: Oxford University Press, 1959), p.117.

[25]See Gabriel Kolko, *Wealth and Power in America: An Analysis of Social Class and Income Distribution* (New York: Praeger, 1964), pp.68 and 127.

[26]Andrew Hacker, *et. al.*, "Corporation, Business", *The New Encyclopaedia Britannica*, 15th ed., vol. 5, p.187.

[27]One percent of all tax-filers in 1960 owned forty-eight percent of all stock held by individuals (Reagan, "What 17 million shareholders share", p.102, cited by Greenberg, *Serving the Few*, New York: John Wiley, 1974, p.45). "In the 150 companies on the current *Fortune* 500 list, controlling ownership rests in the hands of an individual or of the members of a family" (Robert Sheehan, "Proprietors in the World of Big Business", *Fortune*, 15 June 1967, p.179.

[28]See M. U. Chapra, *Towards a Just Monetary System, op. cit.*, pp.110 and 140.

[29]For the definition of these terms within the perspective of *Fiqh*, see Abū Ishāq al-Shāṭibī, *al-Muwāfaqāt fī Uṣūl al-Sharīʿah* (Cairo: al-Maktabah al-Tijāriyyah al-Kubrā, n.d.), vol. 2, pp. 8—12; and Anas Zarqa, "Islamic Economics: An Approach to Human Welfare", *op. cit.*, pp.13—15. Ahmad al-Najjār and Anas Zarqa have, in fact, argued that in the light of Islamic teachings nothing that a man uses (as a consumer or as a producer) is morally free, even if it is economically free (See Ahmad al-Najjār, *al-Madkhal ilā al-Naẓariyyah al-Iqtiṣādiyyah fī al-Islām,* Beirut: Dār al-Fikr, 1973, pp.32 ff; and Anas Zarqa, "Islamic Economics", p.13).

[30]See Thomas McKeown, *The Role of Medicine: Dream, Mirage or Nemesis?* (Princeton, N. J.: Princeton University Press, 1979), and Alastair Gray, "Health and Society: Reflections on Policy", *IDS Bulletin*, October (1983), pp.3—9.

[31]*Majallat al-Ahkām al-ʿAdliyyah*, briefly known as the *Majallah*, states 100 maxims of jurisprudence (*al-qawāʿid al-fiqhiyyah*) in its preamble. An English translation of the *Majallah* by C. R. Tyser, *et. al.* and entitled *The Mejelle* was published in 1967 by All Pakistan Legal Decisions, Nabha Road, Lahore. Although the *Majallah* is a Ḥanafī compendium codified during the Ottoman period, the maxims of jurisprudence are almost universally used by jurists of all schools of Muslim jurisprudence. See also Mustafā A. al-Zarqā, *al-Fiqh al-Islāmī fī Thawbihi al-Jadīd* (Damascus: Maṭābiʿ Alif Bāʾ al-Adīb, 1967), vol. 2, pp. 945—1060. The numbers given within brackets after each principle refer to the articles of the *Majallah* from which the principle has been derived.

[32]See al-Shāṭibī, *al-Muwāfaqāt*, *op. cit.*, vol. 2, p.394; see also Muṣṭafā al-Zarqā, *al-Fiqh al-Islāmī*, *op. cit.*, vol. 2, pp.784 and 1088.

[33]"Most of Pak Funds for Development Misused: Ali Shah Details PAK Findings", summary of a report published on the authority of Reuters by the *Saudi Gazette*, 21 June 1987, p. 7.

[34]In Morocco, only sixteen percent of the subsidy on subsidised foods reached the lowest income group in 1984 (See "World Bank Presents its Six Point Approach to subsidies in Developing Countries", *BIS Review*, 8 April 1987, p.5.

[35]*Ibid.*, pp. 4—6; see also IBRD, *World Development Report 1986*, pp.90—104.

[36]IBRD, *World Development Report 1986*, p.92.

[37]IBRD, *World Development Report 1983*, p.74. The net deficit of a sample of Niger's state-owned enterprises accounted for about four percent of the country's GDP in 1982 (*ibid.*, p.67). Turkish public enterprises averaged net losses equivalent to 3.9 percent of GDP during 1977—9 (*ibid.*, p.74). One study has found that countries in which state-owned enterprises accounted for higher shares of gross domestic investment generally had lower rates of economic growth (see IBRD, *World Development Report, 1987*, pp.66—7).

[38]Although the average defence expenditure of industrial and developing countries was 16.02 percent and 13.16 percent respectively of total government expenditure in 1987, the expenditure of some Muslim countries was: Pakistan, 29.48 percent (1986); Malaysia, 14.38 percent (1987); Egypt, 19.45 percent (1987); Oman, 38.16 percent (1988); and Yemen Arab Republic, 31.21 percent (1988). See IMF, *Government Financial Statistics Yearbook 1989*, pp.58—9.

[39]Paul Kennedy, *The Rise and Fall of the Great Powers: Economic Change and Military Conflict, 1500—2000* (New York: Random House, 1988), pp.XVI and 536—40.

[40]Gunner Myrdal, "Need for Reforms in Underdeveloped Countries", *Quarterly Economic Journal*, National Bank of Pakistan, January—March (1979), p.29.

[41]IMF, *International Financial Statistics, Yearbook 1990*, p.117. The rate of change for Muslim countries is a weighted average calculated from the data on consumer price changes given for twenty-four low- and middle-income Muslim countries in this *Yearbook* (pp. 117—8), and the data for NNP given in World Bank, *World Debt Tables, 1990—1991*.

[42]Calculated from the data given in World Bank, *World Debt Tables, 1990—91*, vols. 1 and 2.

[43]Bukhārī, *al-Jāmi' al-Ṣaḥīḥ*, Kitāb al-Zakāh, "Bāb lā Ṣadaqata illā min Jahri Ghinan"; Abū 'Abd al-Raḥmān ibn Shu'ayb al-Nasā'ī, *Sunan al-Nasā'ī al-Mujtabā*, Kitāb al-Zakāh, "Bāb al-Yadd al-'Ulyā".

[44]See Stephen Fidler, "Third World's Missing Millions", *Financial Times*, 7 September 1987. See also C. L. Ramirez-Rojas, "Monetary Substitution in Developing Countries", *Finance and Development*, June (1986), pp.35–8.

[45]Bukhārī, *Ṣaḥīḥ*, Kitāb al-Ḥarth wa al-Muzāra'ah, "Bāb Faḍl al-Zar' wa al-Ḥarth idhā ukila minhu"; Muslim, *Ṣaḥīḥ*, Kitāb al-Musāqāt, "Bāb Faḍl al-Ghars wa al-Zar'".

[46]Suyūṭī, *al-Jāmi' al-Ṣaghīr* (Cairo: 'Abd al-Ḥamīd Aḥmad Ḥanafī, n.d.), vol. 2, p.167 (see alphabetically under *man bā'a Dāran*), on the authority of Ṭabarānī, the expression within parentheses has been added on the basis of another *ḥadīth* quoted by Suyūṭī on the same page.

[47]M. H. Haykal, *al-Fārūq 'Umar* (Cairo: Maktabah al-Nahḍah al-Miṣriyyah, 1964), vol. 2, p.229.

[48]Muslim, *Ṣaḥīḥ*, Kitāb al-Ḥajj, "Bāb Ḥajj al-Nabī ṣalli Allāh 'alayhi wa sallam".

[49]Abū Yūsuf, *Kharāj*, pp.65–6. This maxim has been introduced in the *Majallah* as Article 97 (see note 31 for an introduction to the *Majallah*).

[50]See article 33 of the *Majallh* (see note 49).

[51]See C. L. Ramires-Rojas, "Monetary Substitutions in Developing Countries", *Finance and Development*, June (1986), p.37.

[52]See OECD, *The Costs of Restructuring Imports — The Automobile Industry* (Paris: OECD, 1987).

[53]IBRD, *World Development Report 1985*, p. 125.

[54]*Ibid.*, p. 129.

[55]This opinion, held by many *fuqahā'*, is based on the Qur'ānic verse related to certain specified items which have been prohibited but the use of which has been allowed in extremely dire circumstances. "He has forbidden carrion, blood, pork and that which has been slaughtered in the name of other than God. However, if one is forced by dire necessity without wilful disobedience or transgression of the limit, no sin shall be on him. Certainly God is Forgiving and Kind" (2:173). There are a number of other verses of this same implication in the Qur'ān (5:3, 6:145, 6:119). By analogy, this principle may be applied to interest paid to foreign lenders with whom no alternative

arrangement is possible, provided that it is resorted to only to the extent absolutely necessary.

[56]See al-Bannā, *Majmū'at Rasā'il, op. cit.*, p.267.

[57]Muhammad Yunus, "The Poor as the Engine of Development", reproduced from *The Washington Quarterly*, Autumn 1987, in *Economic Impact*, 2 (1988), p.31.

[58]Carl Liedholm and Donald Mead, "Small-Scale Enterprise: A Profile", reproduced from their "Small Scale Industries in Developing Countries: Empirical Evidence and Policy Implication", a Michigan State University Development Paper, in *Economic Impact*, 2 (1988), p.12.

[59]An expression of this view appears in International Labour Organisation (ILO), *Employment, Incomes and Equality: A Strategy for Increasing Productive Employment in Kenya* (Geneva: ILO, 1972).

[60]*Report of the Select Committee on Hunger (1986)*, p.4.

[61]Ian Little, Tibor Scitovsky, and Maurice Scott, *Industry and Trade in Some Developing Countries* (London: Oxford University Press, 1970), p.91.

[62]See Mariluz Cortes, Albert Berry and Ashfaq Ishaq, *Success in Small and Medium-Scale Enterprises* (published for the World Bank by Oxford University Press, 1987), p.2.

[63]Liedholm and Mead, "Small Scale Enterprise", *op. cit.*, p. 12.

[64]A number of books have recently been published indicating the strengths of small business. See, for example, Graham Gudgin, *Industrial Location Processes and Employment Growth* (London: Gower, 1978); and David Birch, *The Job Generation Process* (Cambridge, Mass.: M.I.T., Programme on Neighbourhood and Regional Change, 1979); Steven Solomon, *Small Business USA* (New York: Crown Publishers, 1986); David Storey, *et. al.*, *The Performance of Small Firms* (London: Croom Helm, 1987); David J. Storey and Steven G. Johnson, *Job Creation in Small and Medium Sized Enterprises* (Luxembourg: Commission of the European Communities, 1987); and Paul Burns and Jim Dewhurst, *Small Business in Europe* (London: Macmillan, 1987).

[65]*OECD, Employment Outlook* (Paris: OECD, 1986).

[66]Burns and Dewhurst, *Small Business in Europe, op. cit.*, p.193.

[67]See Alan Friedman, "Italian Small Business: The Backbone of the Economy Explored", *Financial Times*, 15 September, 1987.

[68]See "Small Business", *Financial Times*, 29 April 1987, Section III, p. I.

[69]See "Worker-Friendly Programmes", *Economist*, 27 September, 1986, p.20.

[70]Steven Solomon, *Small Business USA, op. cit.*, pp.283–4.

[71]See "Why Japanese Shoppers are Lost in a Maze", *Economist*, 31, January 1987, p.64.

[72]For a discussion of the Japanese profit-sharing system see Martin L. Weitzman, *The Share Economy* (Cambridge, Mass.: Harvard University Press, 1984). It is surprising that while profit-sharing as applied to labour, has attracted attention of the West, profit-sharing as applied to capital, has not attracted such attention. Is it because of cultural myopia or is it because Muslims themselves have not presented the case convincingly?

[73]Paul Baran, *The Political Economy of Growth* (New York: Monthly Review Press, 1957), p.149.

[74]Schumacher, *Small is Beautiful* (London: Blond and Briggs, 1973), p.18.

[75]See the Report by the United Nations' Department of Economic Affairs, *Measures for the Economic Development of Underdeveloped Countries* (New York, 1951), p.29.

[76]Muhammad Yunus, "The Poor as the Engine of Growth", *op. cit.*, p.31.

[77]*Report of the Select Committee on Hunger* (1986), p.V.

[78]Morgan Guarantee Trust Company of New York, *World Financial Markets*, January (1987), p.7.

[79]The non-corporate sector in developing countries generally accounts for 60–70 percent of private sector domestic savings. It is the only sector whose savings exceed its investment (V. V. Bhatt, "Improving the Financial Structure", *Finance and Development*, June (1986), p.20).

[80]Lester Thurow, *Zero-Sum Society* (New York: Basic Books, 1980), p.175.

[81]Quoted by Charles Leadbearer, "Rags to Riches — Fact or Fiction", *Financial Times*, 30 December 1986, p.5.

[82]E. S. Mihshan, *Cost Benefit Analysis: An Introduction* (New York: Praeger, 1971), p.205.

[83]See Alan Friedman "Italian Small Business: The Backbone of the Economy Explored", *Financial Times*, 29 April, 1987, Section III, p. 1.

[84]*Report of the Select Committee on Hunger* (1986), p.4 and chart 2 on p.5.

[85]Loan guarantee schemes exist in practically all industrial countries which, having realised the potential of small firms, have initiated a programme to encourage them. For some relevant details about such schemes in a number of European countries, see Burns and Dawhurst, *Small Business in Europe*, *op.cit.*, pp.199–200.

[86]See *The Economist*, 16 February 1985, p.15.

[87]*Report of the Select Committee on Hunger (1986)*, p.7.

[88]See M. Yunus, "The Poor as the Engine of Growth", *op. cit.*, p.12.

FIVE: WHY THE FAILURE

[1]Ḥasan al-Bannā, *Majmūʻat Rasāʼil*, *op. cit.*, p.255

[2]For the best available analysis of the factors which led to this shift from the system of *shūrā* to hereditary and autocratic rule, see Sayyid Abū al-Aʻlā Mawdūdī, *Khilāfat wa Mulūkiyyat* (Lahore: Islamic Publications, 1966), pp.103–153. See also Sayyid Muḥammad Rashīd Riḍā, *Tafsīr al-Manār* (Cairo: Dār al-Manār, 4th ed., 1954), vol. 4, p.204, and vol. 5, p.198.

[3]From Ibn ʻUmar, in al-Mundhirī, *al-Targhīb wa al-Tarhīb* (Beirut: Dār al-Kutub al-ʻIlmiyyah, 1986), vol. 3, p.155: 1, on the authority of al-Bukhārī and Muslim.

[4]Al-Bukhārī, *Ṣaḥīḥ*, Kitāb al-Aḥkām, from Maʻqil ibn Yasār.

[5]From Abū Saʻīd al-Khudrī, in al-Mundhirī, *al-Targhīb*, *op. cit.*, vol. 3, p.167:7, on the authority of Tirmidhī and Ṭabarānī.

[6]Muslim, *Ṣaḥīḥ*, Kitāb al-Amārah, from Abū Dharr.

[7]The Prophet, may the peace and blessings of God be on him, said: "Faith (*al-dīn*) stands for sincere advice." The Companions inquired: "For whom, O Prophet of God?" The Prophet, peace and blessings of God be upon him, replied: "For God, His Book, His Messenger, the rulers and the common people" (Muslim, *Ṣaḥīḥ*, from Tamīm al-Dārī, Kitāb al-Īmān).

[8]Ibn Hishām, *al-Sīrah al-Nabawiyyah* (Cairo: Maṭabaʻt al-Bābī al-Ḥalabī, 1955), vol. 2, p.661.

[9]Abū Yūsuf, *Kharāj*, *op. cit.*, p.12.

[10]Ibn Taymiyyah, *al-Siyāsah al-Sharʻiyyah fī Iṣlāḥ al-Rāʻī wa al-Raʻiyyah* (Beirut: Dār al-Kutub al-ʻArabiyyah, 1966), p. 135; and Rashid Riḍā, *Manār*, *op. cit.*, vol. 4, p. 45. See also Muhammad Salīm al-ʻAwwā, *Fī al-*

Niẓām al-Siyāsī li al-Dawlah al-Islāmiyyah (Alexandria: al-Maktab al-Miṣrī al-Ḥadīth, 1975), pp.105—17.

[11]Rashid Riḍā, *Manār, op. cit.*, vol. 4, pp.199—200.

[12]See Abū al-A'lā Mawdūdī, *Human Rights in Islam* (Leicester, U.K.: The Islamic Foundation, 1976), p.37.

[13]In this connection, the following *ḥadīth* reported by 'Ā'ishah should be very enlightening. She reports that the Quraysh were faced with the problem of a Makhzūmī lady who had committed theft. They inquired about someone who could intervene on her behalf with the Prophet, may the peace and blessings of God be upon him. They learned that Usāmah ibn Zayd, whom the Prophet, may the peace and blessings of God be upon him, liked very much, may be the only one who could have the courage to do so. Hence Usāmah talked to the Prophet, may the peace and blessings of God be upon him. The Prophet, may the peace and blessings of God be upon him, thereupon said: "Are you intervening to prevent the enforcement of Divine Law?" Then the Prophet, may the peace and blessings of God be upon him, got up and addressed the people saying: "People before you were punished by God because if a highly-placed person stole something they acquitted him, but if a lowly person committed theft they enforced the Law of God on him. By God! Even if Fāṭimah, the daughter of Muhammad, steals, I will certainly cut her hand" (Reported from 'Ā'ishah by al-Bukhārī and Muslim, *Mishkāt al-Maṣābīḥ*, Damascus: al-Maktab al-Islāmī, 1381 A.H., vol. 2, p.302:361).

[14]Rashid Riḍa, *Manār, op. cit.*, vol. 4, p.45.

[15]Ibn Hishām, *Sīrah, op.cit.*, vol. 2, p.661.

[16]See al-Bannā, *Majmū'at Rasā'il, op. cit.*, pp.192—3 and 239—41.

[17]Sayyid Abū al-A'lā Mawdūdī, *The Islamic Law and Constitution* (Lahore: Islamic Publications, 3rd. ed., 1967), p.197.

[18]'Allāl al-Fā'sī, "*al-Islām wa Mutaṭallibāt al-Tanmiyah fī al-Mujtama' al-Yawm*", a paper presented at the conference, "*Multaqā al-Fikr al-Islāmī*", held in Wahrān, July 1971. He argues in favour of the people themselves determining how they wish to be governed. He finds this to be possible only if there is a government by the people's representatives, elected to assemblies by means of free and fair elections, in which the wealthy and the powerful are not able to exercise any pressure or influence (pp. 42—3).

[19]Said the Prophet, may the peace and blessings of God be upon him: "Whoever sees something wrong, should use his strength to set it right; if he cannot, he should speak against it; and if he cannot, he should at least consider it wrong in his heart; and this is the weakest faith" (Muslim,

Ṣaḥīḥ, Kitāb al-Īmān, from Abū Sa'īd al-Khudrī). If this is required of every Muslim, then the obligation of those in positions of influence is much greater.

[20]"Whoever goes along with an oppressor and strengthens his hands, knowing that he is an oppressor, has taken himself out of the fold of Islam" (from Aws ibn Shuraḥbīl, by al-Bayhaqī in his *Shu'ab al-Īmān*; cited in *Mishkāt*, vol. 2, p.641:5136).

[21]From 'Awf ibn Mālik, in al-Mundhirī, *al-Targhīb*, vol. 3, p.175:33, on the authority of al-Bazzār and Ṭabarānī.

SIX: CONCLUSION

[1]K.Ahmad, "Economic Development in an Islamic Framework",in K. Ahmad (ed.), *Studies in Islamic Economics, op. cit.*, p.173. According to Dr. Amin, even the motive for rapid economic development is weak. He says: "Rather than showing a general desire for rapid economic development Arab governments show a surprising weak will to achieve it. . . . A much more powerful motive than economic development is the motive to remain in power" (Galal A. Amin, *The Modernization of Poverty*, vol. VIII of the *Social, Economic and Political Studies of the Middle East* (Leiden: E. J. Brill, 1980), p.108.

★★★

BIBLIOGRAPHY

Abecassis, David, *Identity, Islam and Human Development in Rural Bangladesh* (Dhaka: University Press, 1990).

Ahmad, Khurshid, "Islam and Simple Living", *Criterion* (Karachi), July—August (1970), pp.5—12.

————, "The Third World's Dilemma of Development", *Nonaligned Third World Annual*(1970), pp.3—18.

————, (ed.), *Studies in Islamic Economics* (Leicester, U.K.: The Islamic Foundation, 1980).

Ahmad, Ziauddin, *et al.* (eds.), *Fiscal Policy and Resource Allocation in Islam* (Islamabad: Institute of Policy Studies, 1983).

————, *et al.* (eds.), *Money and Banking in Islam* (Jeddah: International Centre for Research in Islamic Economics, King Abdulaziz University, 1983).

————, *Islam, Poverty and Income Distribution* (Leicester, U.K.: The Islamic Foundation, 1991).

Ahsan, A.S.M. Fakhrul, "Some Issues on the Promotion and Mobilization of Savings Through Islamic Banks", *Thoughts on Economics* (Dhaka) (1987), pp.25—34.

Akkas, S.M. Ali, "Size Distribution of Income and Wealth in an Islamic Economic Framework", *Thoughts on Economics*, 3—4 (1987), pp.68—75.

Alatas, Syed Farid, "An Islamic Common Market and Economic Development", *Islamic Culture*, 1 (1987), pp.28—38.

Ali, A., "The Role of the Islamic Development Bank in the Development Process of Its Member Countries", *Journal of Economic Cooperation Among Islamic Countries* (Ankara), 2 (1989), pp.1—22.

Ali, Abdal Kadir, "Land, Property and Land Tenure in Islam", *Islamic Quarterly* (London), April—July (1959), pp.4—11.

Ali, Ali Abdulla, "How to Reach the Small Farmer: An Islamic Formula", International Foundation for Development Alternatives, Nyon, Switzerland, January—April (1990), pp.35—44.

Amin, Galal A., "The Modernization of Poverty", *Social, Economic and Political Studies of the Middle East* (Leiden: E.J. Brill, 1980), vol. 8.

Ariff, Muhammad, *Monetary and Fiscal Economics of Islam* (Jeddah: International Centre for Research in Islamic Economics, 1982).

Arsalan, Amir Shakib, *Our Decline and its Causes*, tr. M.A. Shakoor (Lahore: S. M. Ashraf, 1962).

El-Ashkar, Ahmad A., "On the Islamic Theory of Consumer Behaviour: An Empirical Inquiry in a Non-Muslim Country", *Arab Banker*, July—August (1986).

————, *The Islamic Business Enterprise* (London: Croom Helm, 1987).

Azam, Khan Muhammad, *Economics and Politics of Development: An Islamic Perspective* (Karachi: Royal Book Co., 1988).

Azid, Toseef, "Unemployment and its Solution in Islam", *Journal of Rural Development and Administration* (Peshawar), 1 (1989), pp.65—77.

Badawi, Jamal A., "Concept of Development from Islamic Perspective", *Al-Nahdah* (Kuala Lumpur), 1 (1989), pp.20—24.

Beg, Tahir, "Economic Development of Indian Muslims: Some Stragetic Options", in Iqbal A. Ansari (ed). *The Muslim Situation in India* (New Delhi: Sterling Publishers, 1989), pp.116—32.

Bianca, Stefano, "Islam and Urban Development", in *Toward Islamization of Disciplines* (Herndon, Va.: The International Institute of Islamic Thought, 1989), pp.297—504.

Chapra, M. Umer, *The Islamic Welfare State and its Role in the Economy* (Leicester, U.K.: The Islamic Foundation, 1979).

————, *Objectives of the Islamic Economic Order* (Leicester, U.K.: The Islamic Foundation 1979).

————, *Towards a Just Monetary System* (Leicester, U.K.: The Islamic Foundation, 1985).

——, *Islam and the Economic Challenge* (Leicester, U.K.: The Islamic Foundation, 1992).

Choudhary, M. Khairat, "Poverty and Income Distribution in Bangladesh", *The Kashmir Economic Review*, July—December (1985), pp.59—72.

——, "The Concept of Islamic Socio-Economic Development in Contemporary Perspective", *The Journal of Development Studies* (1990), pp.1—10.

Esposito, John L., *Islam and Development: Religion and Socio-Political Change* (Syracuse, N.Y.: Syracuse University Press, 1982).

Faridi, F.R., "On Wages in an Islamic Economy", *Islamic Thought* (Aligarh, India), April (1960), pp.61—66.

——, "Fiscal Policy in an Islamic State", *Journal of Research in Islamic Economics*, Summer (1983), pp. 17—35.

Faruqi, Kamal A., "Islam and Social Justice", *Criterion* (Karachi), July—August (1972), pp.34—35.

Gauhar, Altaf, *The Challenge of Islam* (London: Islamic Council of Europe, 1978).

Ghazali, Aidit, *Development: An Islamic Perspective* (Selangor, Malaysia: Pelanduk, 1990).

Ghifari, Nur Muhammad, *Social Security in Islam* (Lahore: Atiq Publication House, 1989).

Gilani, Shaukat J., "The Qur'an on Charitable Giving and Contemporary Social Values", *Journal of Research in Islamic Economics* (1985), pp.63—67.

Government of Pakistan, Federal Bureau of Statistics, *Survey of Social and Economic Impact of Zakat and Ushr on Individual and Household* (Karachi, 1988).

Al-Habshi, Syed Othman, "The Role of Ethics in Economics and Business", *Journal of Islmic Economics* (Malaysia), 1 (1987), pp.1—15.

Haffar, Ahmad R., "Economic Development in Islam in Western Scholarship", *Islam and the Modern Age* (Delhi), May—August (1975).

Hamdulay, Jamaluddin Ahmed, *Islam: The Future Economic System* (Athlone, S.A.: Bookworld Publishers, 1986).

Haniff, Ghulam M., "The Human Resources Path to Development: A Challenge to Muslims", *Islamic Studies*, 2 (1990), pp.131–42.

Haque, Nadeemul and Abbas, Mirakhor "Saving Behaviour in an Economy Without Fixed Interest", *Journal of Islamic Banking and Finance* (Karachi), 3 (1989), pp.24–38.

Hasan, A., "Social Justice in Islam", *Islamic Studies*, 3 (1971), pp.209–19.

Hasanuzzaman, S.M., *The Economic Functions of the Early Islamic State* (Karachi: International Islamic Publishers, 1981).

Holland, Muhtar, *Public Duties in Islam: The Institution of the Hisba* (Leicester, U.K.: The Islamic Foundation, 1982).

Husain, Muzaffar, *Motivation for Economic Achievement in Islam* (Lahore: All Pakistan Educational Congress, 1974).

Hussain, Ch. Muhammad, *Development Planning in an Islamic State* (Karachi: Royal Book Co., 1987).

Ihsanoglu, Ekmeleddin, *Cultural Dimensions of Development in the OIC Member States* (Istanbul: IRCICA, 1991).

International Institute for Labour Studies, *Islam and a New International Economic Order: The Social Dimension* (Geneva: IILs, 1980).

Iqbal, Munawar, *Distributive Justice and Need Fulfilment in an Islamic Economy* (Leicester, U.K.: The Islamic Foundation, 1988).

Islamic Council of Europe, *The Muslim World and the Future Economic Order* (London: Islamic Council of Europe, 1979).

Islahi, Abdul Azim, "Shah Wali Allah's Concept of Al-Irtifaqat: Stages of Socio-Economic Development", *Journal of Objective Studies* (Aligarh, India), 1 (1990), pp.46–63.

Al-Jarhi, Mabid Ali M., "Towards an Islamic Macro Model of Distribution: A Comparative Approach", *Journal of Research in Islamic Economics*, Winter (1985), pp.1–29. See the comment on this by K. A. Naqvi, pp.67–71.

Jarrash, Abdullah Noa'man Al, "Islamic Education for Community Development", *Muslim Education Quarterly* (Cambridge), 4 (1990), pp.36–41.

Johansen, Baber, *The Islamic Law on Land Tax and Rent* (London: Croom Helm, 1987).

Kahf, Monzer, *The Islamic Economy: Analytical Study of the Functioning of the Islamic System* (Plainfield, Indiana: The Muslim Students' Association of the United States and Canada, 1978).

Kazarian, E. and A. Kokko, *Islamic Banking and Development* (Lund: National Ekonomiska Institutionen vid Lunds Universitet, 1987).

Khadduri, Majid, *The Islamic Conception of Justice* (Baltimore: Johns Hopkins University, 1984).

Khan, M. Akram, *Economic Teachings of Prophet Muhammad: A Select Anthology of Hadith Literature on Economics* (Islamabad: International Institute of Islamic Economics, 1989).

———, "Elimination of Poverty in Islamic Economic Framework", *Islamic Studies*, 2 (1990), pp.143—62.

———, *Glossary of Islamic Economics* (London: Mansell, 1990).

Khan, M. Fahim, "Macro Consumption Function in an Islamic Framework", *Journal of Research in Islamic Economics*, Winter (1984), pp. 1—24. See also the comments on this paper by Seif E.I. Tagel-Din, S. Iqbal Mahdi and Zubair Hasan in the Summer (1984) and Winter (1985) issues of this journal, pp.57—61, 73—7 and 79—81 respectively.

———, (ed.), *Distribution in Macroeconomic Framework: An Islamic Perspective* (Islalamabad: International Institute of Islamic Economics, International Islamic University, 1989), pp.111—44.

Llewellyn, Othman A., "Islamic Jurisprudence and Environmental Planning", *Journal of Research in Islamic Economics*, Winter (1984), pp. 25—49. See also the comments on this paper by A. Safi El-Din Awad and the author's rejoinder in the Summer (1985) issue of this journal, pp.83—90.

Majd, Moahmmad G., "Land Reform in Iran", *American Journal of Agricultural Economics*, November (1987), pp.843—48.

Malik, M. Shafi, "Wages in an Islamic Economy", *Islamic Thought* (Aligarh), July (1960), pp.62—67.

Mallat, Chibli (ed.)., *Islamic Law and Finance* (London: Centre of Near and Middle Eastern Studies, School of Oriental and African Studies, 1988).

Mannan, M.A., *Economic Development and Social Peace in Islam* (London: Taha Publishers, 1989).

Mawdudi, Sayyid Abul A'lā, *The Islamic Movement: The Dynamics of Values, Power and Change*, tr. and ed. Khurram Murad (Leicester, U.K.: The Islamic Foundation, 1984).

Meenai, S.A., *The Islamic Development Bank: A Case Study of Islamic Cooperation* (London: Kegan Paul International, 1989).

Mintjes, H., *Social Justice in Islam* (Amsterdam: Institute for the Study of Religion, Free University, 1977).

Muhammad, Yar, *Cooperation Among the Muslim Countries of the World* (Peshawar, Pakistan: Institute of Development Studies, 1987).

Najmabadi, Afsaneh, *Land Reform and Social Change in Iran* (Salt Lake City: Utah University Press, 1988).

Naqvi, S.N.H., "The Margins of State Intervention in an Islamic Economy", *Hamdard Islamicus*, Autumn (1983), pp.47—61.

Nienhaus, Volker, "Economic Development and Islamic Institutions: Islamic Banks and Islamic Common Market", *Bulletin of the Institute of Middle Eastern Studies* (Niigata-Ken, Japan), April (1988), pp.1—26.

Al-Nowaihi, Muhammad, "Fundamentals of Economic Justice in Islam", in *Contemporary Aspects of Economic and Social Thinking in Islam* (Gary, Indiana: MSA, 1973).

Osmani, S.R. and A. Rahman, *Income Distribution in Bangladesh* (New York: United Nations, 1983).

Patel, Zainal Abedin, *Small Kindnesses: Islamic Viewpoint on the Cause and Solution of Global Poverty* (Nuneaton, U.K.: Muslim Venture Publications, 1990).

People Against Interest Debt (PAID), *Usury: The Root Cause of the Injustices — Seminar Transcripts* (Norwich: PAID, 1989).

Pramanik, Ataul Haq, *Economic Development and Distribution in Islam* (London: Grey Seal, 1991).

Qutb, Sayyid, *Social Justice in Islam*, tr. John B. Hardie (Washington, D.C.: American Council of Learned Societies, 1970).

Rahman, Afzalur, *Economic Doctrines of Islam* (Lahore: Islamic Publications, 1975).

Rajab, Ibrahim A., "Islam and Development", *World Development*, vol. 8, pp.513—21.

Rushdi, Ali Ahmad, "The Effects of the Elimination of Riba on Income Distribution", in Munawar Iqbal, *Distributive Justice and Need Fulfilment in an Islamic Economy*, pp.221—50.

Sadeq, A.H.M., *Economic Development in Islam* (Selangor, Malaysia: Pelanduk, 1990).

———, "Islamic Perspectives on Monetary and Fiscal Policies and Implications for Economic Development", *International Journal of Islamic and Arabic Studies* (Bloomington, IN), 1 (1988), pp.1—16.

———, "Mobilization of Resources for Development", *The American Journal of Islamic Social Sciences* (Herndon, VA.), 2 (1989), pp.239—56.

———, et. al. (eds.), *Development and Finance in Islam* (Malaysia: International Islamic University, 1991).

——— (ed.), *Financing Economic Development: Islamic and Mainstream Approaches* (Malaysia: Longman, 1992).

Salahuddin, Muhammad, "Political Obligation: its Scope and Limits in Islamic Political Doctrine", *The American Journal of Islamic Social Sciences*, December (1986), pp.247—64.

Saleh, Nabil A., *Unlawful Gain and Legitimate Profit in Islamic Law: Riba, Gharar and Islamic Banking* (Cambridge: Columbia University press, 1986).

Schirazi, A., *The Problem of Land Reform in the Islamic Republic of Iran: Complications and Consequences of an Islamic Policy* (Berlin: Freie Universitat Berlin, 1987).

Shalaby, Ismail, "The Islamic Common Market", *Journal of Islamic Banking and Finance*, January — March (1988), pp.83—112.

Sharif, M. Raihan, *The Concept of Economic Development in Islam* (Dhaka: Islamic Economics Research Bureau, 1986).

INDEX

★★★